BEGINNING ...Again

Discovering and Delighting
in God's Plan for Your Future

A BIBLE STUDY
WORKBOOK

by Shannon Vowell
featuring the art of Sara Joseph

Sunwing Press

BEGINNING ... *Again*

Discovering and Delighting in God's Plan for Your Future
A Bible Study Workbook

Copyright © 2021 Shannon Vowell

Artwork courtesy Sara Joseph
See more at www.christian-artist-resource.com/sara-joseph.html

All rights reserved. No part of this book may be reproduced, or stored
in a retrieval system, or transmitted in any form or by any means,
electronic, mechanical, photocopying, recording, or otherwise,
without express written permission of the publisher.

ISBN-13: 978-1-7377294-0-2

First Sunwing Press edition
October 2021

Table of Contents

Foreword by Sara Joseph   v

Introduction   1

How to Use This Workbook   4

Week One   **Whose We Are: Father**   7

God is "One", and every person of the Godhead is present in every action. But we want to look closely at Father, Son, and Holy Spirit, to better understand this incredible Triune Lord in Whose image we were made. We begin with Abba. Why? As modern people, we often have serious "authority issues." We have learned to question rules and rule-makers, because they have proven themselves untrustworthy. To receive the peace our Heavenly Father has in mind for us, we need to surrender to the perfect Sovereign Who made us and loves us. He is wise and wonderful and faithful forever!

Week Two   **Whose We Are: Son**   19

It can be so hard to accept the perfect love of Jesus. We struggle to understand how we are "worthy" of salvation; we strive to "earn" what has already been given to us as a gift. Jesus talks tough truth even as Jesus offers incredible mercy and priceless forgiveness; Jesus shows us "the way" even as Jesus Himself IS the Way. Learning to receive and follow Jesus sets us free to live in the fullness of joy He promises us.

Week Three   **Whose We Are: Holy Spirit**   31

Many of us picture God the Father based on artistic representations or a beloved earthly father. Our ideas about Jesus can take their cues from Scripture's description of Him. But how do we understand / visualize God the Holy Spirit? Since Pentecost, God has been present to believers... abiding in us, encouraging us, empowering us, directing us... We are temples of the Holy Spirit. Astonishing.

Week Four   **Where We've Been: Past**   43

As we mark our "Habit Milestone" of 21 days in this study, we apply what we know about our identities as God's children to what we have known about our identities as people in the world. Where are the hurts that need healing? Where are the lies that need correcting? The past does not define us.

Week Five   **Where We Are: Present I**   **59**

Assessing our present state requires a long look in the mirror – of our souls! Are we who we say we are? Are we who we want to be? Where are we succeeding and where do we need help? God delights in our deliverance.

Week Six   **Where We Are: Present II**   **77**

We continue, this week, working to get our arms around the real-life truth of right now. We know this reality is fluid and fragile. We seek the firm foundation of Christ to stabilize all that needs to stay put; we submit to the searching of the Spirit to help us discern all that needs to be set aside, healed, or transformed.

Week Seven   **Why We're Here: Purpose**   **95**

Our study and our practice are showing us ever more clearly: it's not about us. We are not in charge. Only God reigns. But at the same time, we have a very important role to play! This week, we align our personal purpose with God's glorious purposes for us.

Week Eight   **What's Next: Plan**   **111**

Our new habits of prayer, Scripture study, and active servanthood will help us make a plan for the new beginning God has prepared for us. "Commit your work to the Lord, and your plans will be established." (Prov. 16:3) Amen!

Afterword   **126**

Appendix

    A. Suggestions for Group Study   129

    B. Bible Translations and Why They Matter   131

    C. Suggestions for Next Steps   133

About the Author and the Artist   **136**

Foreword

The Source

In an increasingly chaotic world, the gift of a fresh start from One who has the power to make the future extraordinary is a topic that intrigued me. As Shannon points out, opportunities abound for beginning again in just about every aspect of life. It is powerful, transformational renewal that is rare, and only found in a closer walk with Jesus.

I do not doubt that Shannon and I were drawn together by the Holy Spirit. His ability to choreograph details of our lives in rich specificity always astonishes me. Life is, to me, a series of "Aha!" episodes of discovery, as I lurch from stomach churning challenges that stretch me, to unremarkable, bland moments, interspersed with blessings galore and unwanted seasons of enforced rest. His capacity to weave my many muddled moments into significance is unparalleled. Developing the nature of Jesus in me, as in you, is His singular objective.

Shannon and I met because of our mutual passion for the Lord and for beauty. Our paths crossed briefly at a gallery I used to co-own in Dallas, where she purchased some of my work. Years passed before a marketing email from a gallery in Grapevine, featuring my newer work, found its way into her inbox. It became the kindling for reconnecting. This time we had much more in common, more than just our love for shape, color, form and beauty—we had a passion to share the goodness of our God, as discovered in the pages of the Bible.

We intuitively sensed the urgency to get this book into the hands of as many people as possible. Shannon has captured the essence of the quest for recalibrating life, after being shaken. The pandemic of 2020 found us all tossed about like dust motes on a rug. If we are still standing, God must surely have good in store for us!

You are about to begin a journey of discovery, carefully crafted by the Holy Spirit working through Shannon. Ponder the Scriptures she has planted along the way, like blooms whose fragrance must be breathed in slowly. Respond thoughtfully to her insight. I am convinced that the Holy Spirit will guide you on a colorful exploration, traversing landscape you must travel through to arrive at a better destination—the victorious tomorrow of your future!

Document everything because your change and growth will surprise you. Shannon has the gift of asking pertinent questions that invite discovery, whether pleasant or unsettling. Press on. Change will happen effortlessly in the warmth of God's unfathomable love.

The art is my contribution to this endeavor to draw you into quiet places of contemplation. All the paintings were created in my studio, the messy, but sacred place where I commune with Jesus. There, I pester Him with questions, beg for help when I hit unexpected snags and pray, with a brush in my hand and paint on my nose. No subject is off limits. I bring my annoyances, hopes and troubles to Him, as I spread color to bare canvas, or paper, as my mood wills. He is faithful to calm me, laugh at me or laugh with me. He does not hesitate to tell me when I am being melodramatic, while comforting me when my pain is genuine. He is that good!

May the stillness of the landscapes remind you that God is a master of cohesiveness especially in the process of transformation. If He can make something of my messes, He can do much with yours. He will take all the disparate parts of your life's journey and make something of beauty with it. Shannon's writing in this book will help you begin….again, with hope, confidence and strength. Beauty began with God.

—*Sara Joseph*

> The heavens declare the glory of God; the skies proclaim the work of his hands. *–Psalm 19:1*

The New Dawn

> Who will separate us from the love of Christ? Will hardship, or distress, or persecution, or famine, or nakedness, or peril, or sword? As it is written,
>
> > "For your sake we are being killed all day long;
> > we are accounted as sheep to be slaughtered."
>
> No, in all these things we are more than conquerors through him who loved us. For I am convinced that neither death, nor life, nor angels, nor rulers, nor things present, nor things to come, nor powers, nor height, nor depth, nor anything else in all creation, will be able to separate us from the love of God in Christ Jesus our Lord. —*Romans 8:35 - 39*

Proclamation

... My word that goes out from my mouth shall not return to me empty, but it shall accomplish that which I purpose, and succeed in the thing for which I sent it. —Isaiah 55:11

BEGINNING... *Again*

Discovering and Delighting in God's Plan for Your Future

Introduction

"In the beginning..."

Those words speak "being" into existence in a moment.

God breathes all of everything from nothing, suddenly, gloriously! The darkness radiates Light; the void takes on form and substance; Life *begins*...

"In the beginning!"

Every school child knows that a good story has a beginning, a middle, and an end. But the story scripture tells and the stories we live don't conform to that template, do they?

Your attraction to a workbook titled "Beginning ... *Again*" speaks to the fact of tangled-up middles and multiple re-starts in your own story. The pursuit of a good conclusion can necessitate starting over. And starting over. And... well. You know.

We shouldn't be surprised at this pattern. The need to begin again is hardwired into humanity, like the need for oxygen and sleep. God's "new morning mercies" (Lamentations 3:23) exist specifically to meet that need. This is logical, because each of our individual stories mirrors something of the larger story God is telling... and that larger story has hardly begun when it must begin, again, itself.

Recall what happens, directly following "In the beginning..."

The cosmic sweep of Creation and its order and "very goodness" in Genesis 1 gets condensed and concentrated and retold as a specific love story between God and two specific people in a specific place in Genesis 2.

Then that story, too, has to begin again. The ashes of betrayal, shame, innocence soiled and spoiled forever cast Adam and Eve down and out of the Garden, where they try to salvage something of the love they'd lived before by making the first human family (Genesis 3 & 4).

And then that new beginning, too, requires a fresh start – murder and desolation cannot possibly be the end of the story God is telling.

Right from the beginning, new beginnings come thick and fast in scripture. Each is a gift of God's grace; each is costly – sometimes excruciatingly so. Floods and firestorms, occupying armies and exiled prophets, martyrdom and mayhem and all manner of suffering precede the "new morning mercies," every time.

This pattern reaches its pinnacle with Christ – the longed-for Messiah, brutalized and murdered and left for dead before He can be resurrected to reign in perfect, complete, saving love.

Your beginnings... and re-beginnings...

In our own lives as in scripture, new beginnings arrive in rapid succession, right from the start. Childhood, adolescence, adulthood – our lived-out human chronology contains new beginnings as built-in characteristics.

Within that shared chronology, the variety of new beginnings is as broad and deep as the variety of our individual experiences. Is your life the same as everyone who shares your birthday / birthdate? Of course not! Things have *happened* to you; things have *shaped* you. You have experienced change... loss... triumph. You may share your birth-beginning point with millions of people, but no one on earth shares your life experiences in the years since. All of us conform to a general pattern, but each of us lives a completely unique version of it.

That means that the complex story of who you are today is yours alone – distinctive and unrepeatable. It also means the specific motivation behind your desire to make a new beginning today is unique to you. Your reasons for reading these words are your very own. Special. Personal.

But one of the truths spelled out in the "in the beginning..." pages of Genesis is that we humans are made in the image of God. All of us. Our universal attraction to the concept of fresh starts derives from our being made in the image of the One who makes all things new.

> Do not remember the former things,
>   or consider the things of old.
> I am about to do a new thing;
>   now it springs forth, do you not perceive it?
> I will make a way in the wilderness
>   and rivers in the desert.
> —Isaiah 43: 18 - 19

Amazingly, God invites us to fully experience both our universal made-in-God's-image identity *and* our distinctive-and-unrepeatable-personal-story. We don't have to let go of the latter to take hold of the former. Ours is not a "cookie cutter" Creator (as any glimpse of Creation attests)! God's Truth is for *all* of us; God's delight is in *each* of us.

That means that God sees exactly where you are today and knows exactly what you need today and is able to meet you and provide for you in a way that is specifically *for you*... even as God is simultaneously loving and caring for others whose lives and needs are very different from yours. God never runs out of resources, wisdom, or power. And God never stops inviting us to receive those gifts from Him.

If you've been walking with God and these assumptions about Him for a long while already, this workbook is for you.

If you're not sure about God and you have no assumptions whatsoever, this workbook is for you, too.

Full disclosure: I've found myself in both situations. As a child and young adult who knew "God" mostly as a cuss word, I managed multiple forced new beginnings with my own meager resources. I became very good at pretend, denial, and defensiveness. I survived – but I felt like a fraud, always on the verge of being found out. And I dragged all the weight of grief with me into each "new beginning," which made life heavier and harder as the years went by.

More recently, I've navigated some tough new beginnings with the certainty that it was God's strength – not mine – that was carrying me. The freedom to be transparent with Him about just how broken I felt meant that I could receive the help and healing I needed. Because I know myself to be "found" by God, the fear of being "found out" no longer applies. And when I stagger under a burden I cannot bear, I know Who is with me – ready to relieve me and set me on my feet again.

My own experiences make me confident: No matter whether you've chosen your circumstances or they've chosen you, those circumstances are merely the setting for beginning your journey of beginning again. They are *temporary*. Wherever you are at this moment, you will not be here forever, no matter how you feel right now. Best of all, no matter what your track record with new starts is, God will make the difference this time because God IS the story-writer whose narrative of Grace is the larger context for your own life story.

So, for now, we begin. *Again.*

And we ask the One who made us, who has been with us all this time and who will never leave us, to bless our efforts and guide our movements, and to bring glory to His Kingdom, even through us.

Even through our new beginnings.

Breaking Dawn

How to Use This Workbook

We will take 8 weeks to launch our new beginnings, working 5 days a week, 40 days. There are several significant scriptural precedents for 40-day beginnings, and we'll review them. But 8 weeks is also a significant time span from a cognitive / neuropsychological perspective: scientists concur that it takes at least 21 days to form a new habit.

We want the patterns of study, prayer, and action embraced here to become habitual – our new normal. So please embrace this workbook in daily, do-able portions. Holy habits = a life wholly surrendered to God = a holy life. And a holy life contains all the space God needs to make a new beginning beyond anything we can ask or imagine!

*** If you are using this workbook in a small group setting, suggestions for making that process optimal are contained in Appendix A. ***

First Things First

1. **Gather**

   To begin, gather your supplies. You will need not only your workbook, but a good study Bible (see Appendix B for suggestions), a journal, pens and pencils.

2. **Commit**

   If at all possible, designate a space and time for this work. Make it a "standing date" – and honor it as you would a lunch date with a friend. I find that first thing in the morning, while my house is quiet, works best for my devotional work. I like to bring my coffee, light a candle, and snuggle under a favorite blanket while I am working – it translates the spiritual nurturing into physical comfort for me. But whatever works best for you, that should be your routine.

3. **Read**

   Each week, there is a short introduction to read on the evening before you begin the exercises. This introduction will set the tone for the week ahead, naming broad issues, asking some questions-for-thought, and perhaps sharing some quotes.

4. **Organize**

   After the introduction, there will be five days' worth of work, organized "Day 1, Day 2, etc." Your personal calendar may line up so that you read introductions on Sunday evenings, and Monday morning is your Day 1. But that's not a requirement. For example, if you are meeting in a small group on Wednesdays, then you could organize the study so that you read your introductions on Thursday evening and work Friday – Tuesday (so everyone is ready to share on Wednesdays).

There are short teaching segments posted on my website, *shannonvowell.com*, that pertain to each week. These are optional extras, but may enhance your experience. *Bottom line: this is a very flexible format! Make it work for you.*

5. **Complete**

   Each day will have several components to it.

   I. There will be an opening prayer – a long version, and a short / breath prayer version. If you prefer to pray spontaneously, please do! But please read the prayers aloud and allow them to work on your heart, anyway.

   II. There may be a Starting Point question.

   III. There will be several selections of scripture to read.

   IV. There will be a series of questions relating to the scriptures assigned. (There is space in the workbook for responses to the questions, but sometimes you may want to go deeper / write longer – hence the need for a supplementary journal.)

** A word about "Action Items" -- As the study progresses, there will be more frequent, assigned "Action Items"—things to do, to put what you've been thinking about into concrete deeds. Sometimes the Action Item will be easy to accomplish quickly. Sometimes the Action Item will require some effort. Sometimes the Action Item will be watching a movie – takes a while, but no effort involved. The goal is to complete all Action Items as they are assigned, or at least by the end of the work-week, so – again – flexibility is key. Do what you can, when you can. **

A word of encouragement here: whenever we commit ourselves to make a new beginning, there will be voices (in our own heads as well as "out there") telling us that we are fooling ourselves, wasting our time, dooming ourselves to failure, etc.

Those voices need to be acknowledged for what they are: advocates of our continued imprisonment, fighting to hold onto us. Then those voices need to be silenced, so we can tune our ears to the One who beckons us onward. His assurance is vastly more powerful than anything our naysayers can verbalize. He tells us, "I know the plans I have for you. Plans to prosper you and not to harm you. Plans to give you hope and a future." (Jeremiah 29:11)

Whatever ending has brought you to this "Beginning ... *Again*" journey, God sees you right where you are, and God will lead you where you need to go, from there. Blessings to you, every step of the way!

The Planting

....to give unto them beauty for ashes, the oil of joy for mourning,
the garment of praise for the spirit of heaviness; that they might be called trees of righteousness,
the planting of the LORD, that he might be glorified. —Isaiah 61:3

Week One

Whose We Are: Father

God is "One", and every person of the Godhead is present in every action. But we want to look closely at Father, Son, and Holy Spirit, to better understand this incredible Triune Lord in Whose image we were made. We begin with Abba. Why? As modern people, we often have serious "authority issues." We have learned to question rules and rule-makers, because they have proven themselves untrustworthy. To receive the peace our Heavenly Father has in mind for us, we need to surrender to the perfect Sovereign Who made us and loves us. He is wise and wonderful and faithful forever!

Our Starting Point is Abba

Maps and Their Limits

I like to use Google maps on my phone.

I type in the address of where I need to go, and, presto! A map appears right there in the palm of my hand, along with step-by-step instructions for getting from where I am to where I want to be. I can even press a button to translate those instructions into spoken directions, so that I can drive while my phone tells me what to do next.

My children are not nearly as bedazzled as I am by this technology. They have grown up with it, and find it almost incomprehensible that when I was their age I wrote down directions on a piece of paper and / or used a folding map to get from point A to point B. And that I did this (and everything else in life) without use of a phone… unless I stopped and used a "payphone" (like in the old Superman movies).

My husband can't use Google maps like I do. That's because he has disabled the automatic location function on his phone. A former military officer, he is not comfortable with apps tracing his every move, and being "off grid" is, to him, worth the trouble of needing to stop for directions occasionally. Notice that his phone is useless for finding his way because Google maps (or any digital direction service) only works if the phone's location can be pinpointed as a starting point.

In that respect, navigation hasn't changed from the paper map days. You have to know your beginning point before you can accurately figure your trajectory. That's true whether you're punching an address into a phone or looking for a dot on a paper map. Knowing where you want to go is only half the equation – you have to know where you're starting from, too. And no matter how you figure the navigation, the only place you can begin from is where you are.

We are embarking on a journey together – we are "beginning... *again*" – and we know that we want to get somewhere. We know we want somewhere else – somewhere fresh and clean and whole – somewhere other than where we are. But how do we assess where we are, so that we can chart a course?

Maps and the Maker

Scripture tells us that we are, in our deepest and most eternally stable core, creations of the Creator – made in the image of the One True God. Scripture describes God making us, breathing life into us, calling us "very good", giving us work and purpose as well as form. We were made by God. And we were also made *like* God – in God's image.

Therefore, we cannot know ourselves unless we know the One in whose image we are made. And we cannot figure out either where we are or where we're wanting to go until we have a basic grasp of Whose we are, for two reasons.

First, because God's is the only Way that reliably meets us right here (wherever "here" may be).

Second, because God's Way is also the only route that reliably takes us home to Heaven by way of fulfillment, purpose, and peace.

Therefore, pinpointing our present location on the map of our lives – as well as charting the course of our new beginning – must commence with a review of the One True God.

Mapping for Accuracy

When I was a new Christian, I was confused by people who talked about God as if He had a split personality. The "angry God" of the Old Testament was someone distinct from "gentle Jesus, meek and mild", some insisted. They rejected the former as a harsh, condemning Angry Man, and embraced the latter as a kind of Embodiment of Universal Affirmation. Old Testament God: Bad; New Testament God: Good.

Say, what?!

During my husband's years as a Naval Flight Officer, he navigated planes' routes based on fixed points outside the plane. Sometimes those points were geographic elements – a mountain, a bridge, a light house. Over open ocean, those points were stars. Accurate calculations for a flight path depended on these fixed points. The quickest way to get off track was to "buy a bad fix" – to calculate based on wrong information regarding those fixed points. Buy a bad fix, and there's no way to arrive at your destination.

When we think of God as a splintered, schizophrenic character, we are buying a bad fix. We can't possible navigate accurately based on bad data about God.

Further, misunderstandings in this category create all kinds of traps for us – because denying the truth of God's identity as revealed in scripture sets us up to trip over everything else. Careful reading corrects us. When we read carefully, we find there is no "good cop / bad cop" paradigm in the person of God. Rather, there is seamless wholeness and holiness, manifested across the eons.

Specifically, the actions of the Father in the Old Testament find their fulfillment in the saving action of the Son in the New.

Beyond that cooperation within history, Father and Son exist outside of history – in an eternal relationship of reciprocal love.

God's consistent goodness has to be the fixed point from which we calculate our flight path, or we will arrive at inhospitable places ad infinitum.

Compass Corrective

Jesus called God, the Father, "Abba." Roughly translated into modern English, Abba means "Daddy." The Son's words and works reveal the Father in all His multi-faceted glory: infinite strength alongside infinite tenderness motivated by infinite love.

But it's important to acknowledge a common navigational error at this point: mistaking our Father in Heaven for a large-scale version of our own fathers. At their best, earthly fathers point us to God through their love, their strength, their protective instincts and their faithfulness as providers. But sometimes our experience of earthly fathers renders ludicrous the idea of a Good Father in Heaven.

Being abandoned by an earthly father makes one suspicious of the supposed faithfulness of God. Being abused by an earthly father makes one suspicious of God's purported kindness. Watching an earthly father repeatedly make stupid mistakes or fall victim to addiction makes one skeptical of the very notions of wisdom and purity – and therefore unable to accept that God is both perfectly wise and perfectly holy.

Sadly, some of us hear "Father" and instinctively flinch – or run.

If your experience of earthly fatherhood has left you wounded and cynical, I encourage you to resist the urge to assume God the Father is just like your dad. God's version of paternity is flawless and faithful. And God persists in patiently seeking the healing and welfare of all of His children... including you.

Don't take my word for it, but please do take *His*, this week.

So, our journey begins with God, the Father, our Abba.

As we pray, study, and work this week, we will seek to understand who God, the Father is – how God, the Father, interacts with us – and why we are blessed to be called children of God, the Father.

> Yet you, Lord, are our Father.
> We are the clay, you are the potter;
> we are all the work of your hand.
> —Isaiah 64:8

Breaking Forth

God the Father

Week One Prayers

From Matthew 6:9 - 13

Our Father, who art in heaven,
  hallowed be thy name.

Thy kingdom come.
  Thy will be done,
    on earth as it is in heaven.

Give us this day our daily bread.
  And forgive us our trespasses,
    as we forgive those who trespass against us.

And lead us not into temptation,
  but deliver us from evil.

For thine is the kingdom,
  and the power, and the glory forever.

Amen

Breath Prayer Version

Inhale: God, you are my Holy Father;

Exhale: Thy will be done, even in me.

WEEK ONE ACTION ITEMS

Weekly Tasks

1. Remember to view the introduction for this week which is available for you at shannonvowell.com.

2. Please serve someone in a position of authority (pastor, police, doctor, teacher, boss, etc.) at least once this week. Consider writing a note, sending flowers, bringing a meaningful gift. Thank him / her for using authority to bless others.

Daily Gratitude List

List two things for which you are grateful... & then acknowledge each thing as *a gift from God*, the Father, "giver of all good gifts" (James 1:17).

As you prepare for this week's work, please think about the following questions and familiarize yourself with this week's model prayer and action item(s).

1. Whose authority are you under? Why? What are the conditions? (For example, under the authority of your boss at work, the traffic cop when you drive, the IRS when you file taxes, etc.)

2. How does being "under authority" affect you?

3. When / how have authority figures in your life let you down? When / how have authority figures in your life provided you with protection and guidance?

Day 1

READ Genesis 1:1 – Genesis 2:4; Isaiah 49:15 - 16

What does it mean to you that God is the author of all Creation?

What does it mean to you that you are made "in God's image"?

What does it mean to you that God's charge to humankind is to be in authority over Creation?

How does all this connect with the image of your name engraved in the palm of God's hand? Discuss.

Today, I am grateful to God the Father for

1.

2.

Today, I served / plan to serve

Breath Prayer

God, you are my Holy Father;

Thy will be done, even in me.

Day 2

READ   Deuteronomy 5:6 – 7; 6:4 – 12; 10:12 – 11:1

In these passages, what is the basis of God's authority as the law-giver?

What is the relationship between God and the people of Israel, and how does God's authority shape that relationship?

When you consider your own relationship with God, to what extent is God's authority the shaping influence?

If you see other things as more prominent, name and discuss them.

*Today, I am grateful to
        God the Father for*

1.

2.

Today, I served / plan to serve

> **Breath Prayer**
>
> God, you are my Holy Father;
>
> Thy will be done, even in me.

Day 3

READ Psalm 8; Psalm 18:1 – 19; Psalm 29; Psalm 145:1 – 13

Where does the psalmist see God's authority manifested in Creation?

Where do you see God's authority manifested in Creation?

What connections do you see between order, balance, beauty, and authority – based on these psalms and on Creation itself? Discuss.

Today, I am grateful to
God the Father for

1.

2.

Today, I served / plan to serve

Breath Prayer

God, you are my Holy Father;

Thy will be done, even in me.

Day 4

READ Proverbs 3:1 – 12; Isaiah 55; Matthew 17:1 - 8

What are some commands God makes in these scriptures?

What are some promises God makes?

How are the commands and promises connected?

Consider: God's authority gives God the right to give commandments. God's authority also gives God the ability to keep promises. Why is authority so integral to God's goodness and power?

*Today, I am grateful to
    God the Father for*

1.

2.

Today, I served / plan to serve

> *Breath Prayer*
>
> God, you are my Holy Father;
> Thy will be done, even in me.

Day 5

READ John 17

How does Jesus acknowledge and honor the authority of the Father in this prayer?

In the prayer, how does God's authority radically impact your personal status? (Hint: look for descriptions of unity...)

What does this prayer mean for you, personally, in terms of your own authority to impact the world as one claimed and empowered by God?

*Today, I am grateful to
   God the Father for*

1.

2.

Today, I served / plan to serve

> **Breath Prayer**
>
> God, you are my Holy Father;
>
> Thy will be done, even in me.

The Meeting Place

I am the way, and the truth, and the life. No one comes to the Father except through me.
—John 14:6

Week Two

Whose We Are: Son

It can be so hard to accept the perfect love of Jesus. We struggle to understand how we are "worthy" of salvation; we strive to "earn" what has already been given to us as a gift. Jesus talks tough truth even as Jesus offers incredible mercy and priceless forgiveness; Jesus shows us "the way" even as Jesus Himself IS the Way. Learning to receive and follow Jesus sets us free to live in the fullness of joy He promises us.

Jesus: Man, Myth, Legend, Lord!

Before I became a Christian, I heard many weird and contradictory things about Jesus. Frankly, the "good cop / bad cop" malarky about God generally was applied in all sorts of specific ways to Jesus, the Son and Savior. Claims about Jesus were so all over the map that I had to take a deep breath before I sat down to the gospels to investigate for myself.

"Bad Fixes" re: our Messiah

See if you've heard – and scratched your head – over any of these claims:

- Jesus is the ultimate pacifist, so meek and mild that he wouldn't say "boo" to a goose. But also, Jesus has "anger issues" – indulging in public temper tantrums and destruction of private property; saying rude things to his closest friends.

- Jesus has been grossly misrepresented by naïve supporters. They say he worked miracles, but since miracles are technically impossible, we all know the miracle-stories were added into scripture later – by those naïve supporters. People promoting the "Jesus myth." Whatever *that* is.

- Jesus was God's precious little baby boy, and God sent him to suffer and die on the cross because I am such a bad person. (Say, what?!)

- Jesus was an amazing teacher of morals and a gentle champion of the poor. Nothing more.

- Jesus was an idea. A beautiful idea. Kind of like… Santa Claus.

When I finally read the gospels for myself, I discovered that all those wacky claims had vague associations with the reality of Jesus, but that none of them had anything to do with the truth of Jesus. Bottom line, Jesus was not just completely different than the wacky misrepresentations I'd heard, Jesus was also *so much more* than anyone had ever told me.

Accurate headings, from the Source Himself

We'll be taking an extended, intensive look at Jesus this week. But let's begin with some background information straight (if you'll forgive me the colloquialism) from the horse's mouth. Here's what *Jesus* had to say on the topic of His identity and purpose:

> **I am the bread of life. He who comes to Me shall never hunger, and he who believes in Me shall never thirst.** *–John 6:35*
>
> **I am the light of the world. He who follows Me shall not walk in darkness, but have the light of life.** *–John 8:12*
>
> **I am the door. If anyone enters by Me, he will be saved, and will go in and out and find pasture.** *–John 10:9*
>
> **I am the good shepherd. The good shepherd gives His life for the sheep.** *–John 10:11*
>
> **I am the resurrection and the life. He who believes in Me, though he may die, he shall live.** *–John 11:25*
>
> **I am the way, the truth, and the life. No one comes to the Father except through Me.** *–John 14:6*
>
> **I am the true vine, and My Father is the vinedresser.** *–John 15:1*
>
> **Truly, truly, I say to you, before Abraham was, I am.** *–John 8:58*

Sustenance. Light. Truth. Protection. Guidance. Source. Eternal Life. Jesus articulates huge claims in small sentences and keeps his language clear, so there's no way we can misunderstand Him. These statements beg the question, "How have people stayed confused about Jesus for over two millennia, given how straightforward Jesus, Himself, was?"

Our goal this week is to refuse the rumors and get crystal clear about Jesus. If we are beginning again, and if Jesus is our Savior in that process as in all of life, then we need to really know who Jesus is – and what He is not!

I'd like to share with you a lovely allegory of the Who / How / Why of Jesus. Popularized by 20th century journalist Paul Harvey, this sweet little story is a favorite of mine.

Savior

Once there was a man who did not believe in God. He was a kind man. He loved his wife and children. He worked hard. He didn't mind that his wife took their children to church; if it made them happy, why would he object?

One Christmas Eve, the man was home alone while his family was attending candlelight worship. It was a bitter cold night; the weather forecast predicted temperatures would continue to fall. The man had tried to persuade his family that perhaps this year it would be a good idea to skip Christmas worship. After all, the weather was bad and getting worse; was it worth the risk?

"Jesus came to rescue us, dear, "his wife had explained. "Jesus became human for our sake, so we could be saved. Going to worship him isn't a risk – it's a pleasure."

As the man waited for his family to get home, he mulled over what his wife had said. Why would God need to rescue people? And why would God need to become human to do it? It made no sense.

Looking outside, the man noticed a small flock of birds, huddled miserably on the power line. "They will freeze to death," he said to himself. What could he do to help them?

Suddenly inspired, the man bundled up and went outside. He opened the door to his garage, just below where the birds were huddled. It was warm inside, and there was shelter from the freezing rain that had begun to fall. But the birds didn't move.

"Shoo, birds!" The man called. "Go inside!" The birds didn't move.

Frustrated, the man waved his arms and shouted at the birds. They fluttered a short distance, but landed again on the power line – fully exposed to the rain and the murderous cold.

Shivering, the man went back into his house. He stood at the window and watched the little flock of birds through the rain that was falling harder now, freezing into pellets of ice.

"If only I could help them," the man thought to himself. "If only I could communicate to them that they would be safe and warm in the garage – that they would make it through this storm if they would just take shelter."

The stupidity of the birds and their helplessness and vulnerability frustrated the man. He stood at the window, watching and fretting.

After a while, the man smiled sadly. "If I were a bird, " he thought, "I would lead them into the garage. If I were a bird, they would trust me and follow me, and they would be saved."

At that moment, the man heard church bells ringing through the storm.

"Jesus," he said aloud, falling to his knees, "I see it now. I see it now!"

God the Son

Week Two Prayers

Jesus, the Good Shepherd, Psalm 23

The Lord *is* my shepherd;
I shall not want.
He makes me to lie down in green pastures;
He leads me beside the still waters.
He restores my soul;
He leads me in the paths of righteousness
For His name's sake.
Yea, though I walk through the valley of the shadow of death,
I will fear no evil;
For You *are* with me;
Your rod and Your staff, they comfort me.
You prepare a table before me in the presence of my enemies;
You anoint my head with oil;
My cup runs over.
Surely goodness and mercy shall follow me
All the days of my life;
And I will dwell in the house of the Lord forever.

Breath Prayer Version

Inhale: Lord Jesus Christ, Holy Son of God, my Shepherd…

Exhale: Have mercy on me – your wandering, wondering sheep.

WEEK TWO ACTION ITEMS

Weekly Tasks

1. View this week's introduction video at shannonvowell.com.

2. Serve someone who is directly involved in caring for, serving, or helping heal other people (medical professionals, home health providers, moms of young children, preschool teachers & nursery workers, counselors, pastors, janitors / custodial service workers, etc.) – note, call, gift, etc. – at least once this week.

3. Do something that falls into the "foot washing" category for you, personally. (Grocery shopping. Bathroom cleaning. Laundry. Errands. Whatever feels "beneath you," stoop to do it as an act of worship of Jesus.) Do this at least once this week.

Daily Gratitude List

List two things every day for which you are grateful, and then *acknowledge the "greatest gift" – salvation in Jesus Christ – as your third item every day.*

As you prepare for this week's work, please answer the following questions and familiarize yourself with this week's model prayer and action item(s).

1. What does it mean to be "saved"? Are you "saved"? Why / why not? Does it matter? Why / why not?

2. What kinds of rumors and contradictory accounts of Jesus have affected your faith walk?

Day 1

READ John 1:1 – 18; John 3:16 – 21; John 13:1 – 17

Based on John chapter 1, who is Jesus?

Based on John chapter 3, who is Jesus?

Based on John chapter 13, who is Jesus?

Which of these aspects of Jesus's identity have you experienced personally? How?

Which of these aspects of Jesus's identity have you witnessed in the character of Christians? Describe that.

Based on these readings, are there ways in which Christians have mis-represented Jesus to you? Discuss.

Today, I am grateful to God the Father for

1.

2.

3.

Today, I served / plan to serve

> *Breath Prayer*
>
> Lord Jesus Christ, Holy Son of God, my Shepherd…
>
> Have mercy on me – your wandering, wondering sheep.

Day 2

READ   Matthew 1:18 – 25, Matthew 7:13 – 29, Matthew 8:23 – 34

How does the angel describe Jesus to Joseph? What is Jesus's purpose, according to Matthew 1?

How does this purpose intersect with Jesus's own teaching in Matthew 7?

What does the account of Jesus's miraculous power of both nature (storms at sea) and evil (demons who have possessed humans) in Matthew 8 add to this understanding of Jesus?

Think about the reaction of the community of the Gadarenes. Why do you think they asked Jesus to leave their region?

Today, I am grateful to God the Father for

1.

2.

3.

Today, I served / plan to serve

> **Breath Prayer**
>
> Lord Jesus Christ, Holy Son of God, my Shepherd…
>
> Have mercy on me – your wandering, wondering sheep.

Day 3

READ   Luke 5:17 – 26, Luke 6:6 – 11, Luke 7:18 – 23, Luke 10:25 – 37

According to Jesus, which requires more authority – healing physical infirmity or forgiving sin?

What point is Jesus making when He heals the man on the sabbath? How / does this amplify his point with the paralytic?

In Luke 7, how does Jesus identify himself to John the Baptist's disciples?

What does the parable of the Good Samaritan tell you about Jesus's "categories" for people?

*Today, I am grateful to
    God the Father for*

1.

2.

3.

Today, I served / plan to serve

> **Breath Prayer**
>
> Lord Jesus Christ, Holy Son of God, my Shepherd…
>
> Have mercy on me – your wandering, wondering sheep.

Day 4

READ   Mark 5:21 – 43, Mark 7:24 – 30, Mark 10:13 – 16

In these passages in Mark, Jesus singles out people whom that culture would designate as "less than." Women, generally, were not seen as equal to men; children were property; and foreigners ("Syro-phoenician") were doubly-less-deserving. What do you notice about the way Jesus deals with such people?

Given the prejudices of His time, what does this behavior tell you about Jesus?

What are some prejudices of your times? How might Jesus deal with them?

Consider Jesus's standard of having "faith like a little child" to enter the Kingdom of Heaven. What do you need to work on?

Today, I am grateful to God the Father for

1.
2.
3.

Today, I served / plan to serve

> **Breath Prayer**
>
> Lord Jesus Christ, Holy Son of God, my Shepherd...
>
> Have mercy on me – your wandering, wondering sheep.

Day 5

READ Philippians 2:5 – 11, 1 Peter 1:3 – 9, 1 John 2:1 – 6

First, take a moment to think about the experience of the men who wrote these letters:

Paul, who viciously persecuted the church until Jesus knocked him off his horse on the Damascus Road!

Peter, who denied Jesus three times on the night before Jesus went to the cross, but became the "rock" on which Christ built the church!

John, the beloved disciple, who out-lived all the other eyewitnesses of Jesus and called himself "the disciple Jesus loved"!

Now, describe the impact of these words on you *in light of WHO these writers were and HOW they knew Jesus.*

How does your own story impact the way you talk about Jesus? Discuss.

Today, I am grateful to God the Father for

1.

2.

3.

Today, I served / plan to serve

> **Breath Prayer**
>
> Lord Jesus Christ, Holy Son of God, my Shepherd…
>
> Have mercy on me – your wandering, wondering sheep.

Fishermen on the Galilee

Called By Jesus

Look back over your notes from this week.
Have you learned anything new about Jesus?
Have you had any ideas challenged or changed?

Making a Stir

*Now the earth was formless and empty, darkness was over the surface of the deep,
and the Spirit of God was hovering over the waters.* —Genesis 1:2

*When all the people were being baptised, Jesus was baptised too. And as he was praying,
heaven was opened and the Holy Spirit descended on him in bodily form like a dove.* —Luke 3:22

Week Three

Whose We Are: Holy Spirit

Many of us picture God the Father based on artistic representations or a beloved earthly father. Our ideas about Jesus can take their cues from Scripture's description of Him. But how do we understand / visualize God the Holy Spirit? Since Pentecost, God has been present to believers… abiding in us, encouraging us, empowering us, directing us… We are temples of the Holy Spirit. Astonishing.

The Breath of God

As a new believer, getting to know the basics of the Father and Jesus was mostly a matter of time in scripture. Learning the truth of the character of the One God as expressed in those two Persons – that was a joyful adventure of discovery for this book-nerd.

But the Holy Spirit? It seemed to me there was no coming to grips with a Person of the Godhead who wasn't, well, a *person*.

It didn't help that my first Bible was an older translation, in which "Holy Spirit" appeared as "Holy Ghost." A bad habit of horror-movie-watching when I was a teenager predisposed me to cover my eyes at the mention of anything "ghostly". Honestly, I wasn't sure I wanted to get better acquainted with this aspect of God.

Beyond my ghoulish, "things that go bump in the night" phobia about ghosts, I struggled with the concept of "spirit". I discovered that the Greek word for "spirit" was the same as the word for "breath" – *pneuma*, from which we get our English "pneumonia." My sister had almost died of pneumonia when we were young. Why would I want to get to know God in the guise of collapsed lungs?!

Bottom line, the Holy Spirit seemed to me both nebulously scary and completely confusing.

At such places of fear and confusion, I find that **gravity** helps me a lot.

How so? Because I don't "get" gravity, either. I don't understand the principles by which I stay fixed to the surface of a planet that is whirling through space. I don't understand why rockets have to "break free" from the atmosphere, nor why astronauts weigh less on the moon. The whole thing mystifies me… and totally freaks me out if I think about it too much.

Gravity goes on holding me to earth, though. My comprehension has no bearing whatsoever on its efficacy; me freaking out matters not a whit.

Like gravity, God keeps working perfectly without my comprehension (or my permission).

Even better, neither God nor gravity relies on me. For anything. But both God and gravity can be relied on, by me, even in the absence of my "getting" them. What a relief!

In fact, in the un-gettable-ness of God, I have an ongoing reminder of my true identity: God's child, not "god" myself. I am not responsible for the Universe. I cannot "save" anyone – not even myself – but that's not my job. When I put my trust in the goodness of the God I cannot comprehend, that place of surrender becomes my custom-fit haven. Rather like this planet, onto which gravity holds me so faithfully, is my custom-fit home.

The liberating truth is that I am not going to fly off into outer space, because I am held safely by the One who made me, and gravity, and outer space, and everything!

> For in him all things were created: things in heaven and on earth, visible and invisible, whether thrones or powers or rulers or authorities; all things have been created through him and for him. *–Colossians 1:16*

If gravity has the power to hold us secure on terra firma, the Holy Spirit has the power to lift us to heavenly heights at the same time. Gravity exerts "natural" power; the Holy Spirit *is* supernatural power. Gravity keeps us physically anchored in the present moment; the Holy Spirit gives us glimpses of eternity and empowers us to live "now" with the "not yet" resident in our very beings.

We see this power especially clearly when the Holy Spirit catalyzes transformation in disciples of Jesus at Pentecost. The second chapter of Acts contains so much that is startling that it's easy to miss the central miracle: Peter, the cowardly Christ-denier, preaching the gospel to a crowd of thousands in the very city where his Lord had been condemned! The Holy Spirit falling on him had not just loosened his tongue to miraculously speak in other languages – the Holy Spirit had redefined his identity: terrified fisherman to fearless apologist.

The apostle Paul's transformation – from malevolent persecutor of Christians to church-planting / New Testament martyr for the faith – follows soon thereafter (in Acts 9).

These two men's experiences exemplify the action of the Holy Spirit in the lives of believers: unmistakable change, undeniable urgency, inexplicable effectiveness – supernaturally.

Those who claim that such miracles of transformation are no longer part of Christian experience are missing out on God's gifts. Lives are still changed, in ways just as radical as Peter and Paul's! Here are a few examples from my own acquaintanceship: my friend Bob, who went from sleeping off Saturday nights every Sunday morning to leading ministries at his church; my friend Lisa, whose legendary sharp tongue and bitter mindset were replaced by sparkle-eyed kindness and evangelical energy; my friend Don, whose decades of alcoholism almost killed him but who walks now in a sobriety so joyful and Jesus-focused that he inspires other long-time drunks to give God a try. These are real people, living in real freedom, thanks to the reality of the Holy Spirit!

Paul encourages disciples not to be "conformed" to the pattern of the world, but rather to be "transformed" by the renewing of our minds. (Romans 12:2) Only the Holy Spirit can enable us (as Paul was enabled) to believe that such transformation is possible. And only the Holy Spirit can enable us (as Peter, Paul, and countless others have been enabled) to live into that amazing paradigm of supernatural change.

The "breath prayers" we've been saying for the last two weeks constitute a Holy Spirit habit. By syncing our breathing with our words of prayer, we are living into the "pneuma" of God intentionally and specifically. I encourage you to actively picture your lungs being filled with the Holy Spirit as you pray this week. Recall God, in Creation, breathing into Adam's nostrils... and be reminded that every single breath is a gift from God to you. The Holy Spirit is power! And the Holy Spirit is literally as close as your next breath.

> By the word of the Lord the heavens were made,
> and all their host by the breath of his mouth. *–Psalm 33:6*

God the Holy Spirit

Week Three Prayers

Adaptation of the Serenity Prayer by Reinhold Niebuhr

Holy Spirit, grant me serenity… to accept the things I cannot change.

Holy Spirit, fuel me with courage… to change the things I can.

Holy Spirit, endow me with Your wisdom. Show me clearly where I am to act and where I am to wait on Your action.

Holy Spirit, empower me to live one day at a time, to enjoy one moment at a time, and to accept one hardship at a time.

Holy Spirit, abide in me, I pray. In Your abiding presence, make my trust steadfast and my surrender to Your will complete.

Holy Spirit, bring Your fruit forth from my character.

And Holy Spirit, keep me mindful that the day is coming when I will be perfectly happy and eternally secure in Your full physical presence, forever and ever!

Amen.

Breath Prayer Version

Inhale: Holy Spirit, abide in me and make me Yours, I pray…

Exhale: Holy Spirit, breathe in me and bring me life in You.

WEEK THREE ACTION ITEMS

Weekly Tasks

1. View this week's introduction video at shannonvowell.com.

2. "Dance before the Lord" like King David (2 Samuel 6:14 – 15) at least once this week. Focus on committing your whole body to praising God. (I realize this can be way uncomfortable and feel really goofy, but please do whatever you need to do to put yourself in position to give it a real try.) Play your favorite Christian music loudly, and offer God your best moves, in worship!

3. Look back at the weekly tasks for the first two weeks. Choose one (serving an authority figure, serving a caretaker, performing a foot-washing task) and do it at least once this week.

Daily Task

Make time to enjoy Christian music that connects you with the Holy Spirit. It may be an old-fashioned hymn or the latest contemporary praise ballad, but focus specifically on the music and the Spirit for the duration of at least one whole song each day.

Daily Gratitude List

List three things every day for which you are grateful, noting that they are gifts from the Father. Acknowledge the "greatest gift" – salvation in Jesus Christ – as a fourth item every day. And give thanks for the gift of the Holy Spirit abiding in you as your fifth / final list item.

As you prepare for this week's work, please answer the following questions and familiarize yourself with this week's model prayer and action item(s).

1. What aspects of your life / faith do you perceive as beyond the possibility of change? Why are these aspects entrenched?

2. Have you ever witnessed or experienced a miracle? If so, describe it below. If not, describe your attitude toward miracles in the present day.

Day 1

READ   1 John 4:13; John 14:26, 15:26; Acts 1:1 – 5; 2:1 – 4, 43 – 47

According to these scriptures, who sends the Holy Spirit, and why?

What does the Holy Spirit have to do with Jesus's ministry?

What happened at Pentecost? Based on Acts 2:43 – 47, what was the result?

How do you experience the Holy Spirit in your worship? Prayer life? Daily routine? Discuss.

Today, I am grateful to God for

1.
2.
3.
*4.
*5.

Today, I served / plan to serve

Today, I worshiped the Holy Spirit through this music

Breath Prayer

Holy Spirit, abide in me and make me yours, I pray…

Holy Spirit, breathe in me and bring me life in You.

Day 2

READ 2 Samuel 23:1 – 2; Proverbs 3:13 – 26; Isaiah 63:7 – 14; Mark 13:9 – 11

What are some implications of these Old Testament references to the Holy Spirit?

What do Jesus's words to his disciples in Mark's gospel add to the Old Testament teachings?

Does any of this apply to you / your life? Discuss.

Today, I am grateful to God for

1.

2.

3.

*4.

*5.

Today, I served / plan to serve

Today, I worshiped the Holy Spirit through this music

> **Breath Prayer**
>
> Holy Spirit, abide in me and make me yours, I pray...
>
> Holy Spirit, breathe in me and bring me life in You.

Day 3

READ Romans 8:1 – 17; 1 Corinthians 12:1 – 13

Paul speaks to the work of the Spirit in individuals (Romans) and in Christ's body, the church (1 Corinthians). List the teachings Paul offers.

The Spirit in Individuals: The Spirit in Community:

Looking at your lists, think about your personal experience and your experience in Christian community. Where have you seen the Holy Spirit at work?

Write a prayer asking the Holy Spirit to fill in any gaps and dazzle you with revival!

Today, I am grateful to God for

1.
2.
3.
*4.
*5.

Today, I served / plan to serve

Today, I worshiped the Holy Spirit through this music

Breath Prayer

Holy Spirit, abide in me and make me yours, I pray...

Holy Spirit, breathe in me and bring me life in You.

Day 4

READ Galatians 5:22 – 23; John 15:1 – 5; Matthew 7:15 – 20

Meditate on the famous verse from Galatians regarding the "Fruit of the Spirit." What do you notice?

According to Jesus's teaching in John's gospel, what makes us fruitful? How does this connect to the Galatians verse?

According to Jesus's teaching in Matthew's gospel, what is the significance of fruitfulness in a believer's life? How does this connect to the Galatians verse?

Today, I am grateful to God for

1.
2.
3.
*4.
*5.

Today, I served / plan to serve

Today, I worshiped the Holy Spirit through this music

Breath Prayer

Holy Spirit, abide in me and make me yours, I pray...

Holy Spirit, breathe in me and bring me life in You.

Day 5

READ ALOUD Acts 7:55 – 56; Revelation 1:1 – 18; 21:1 – 7

In your own words, describe what Stephen saw.

What does it mean to you that he was "filled with the Holy Spirit" when he saw what he did?

Picture the apostle John alone, in exile on the island of Patmos. His vision here begins with his "being in the Spirit on the Lord's day." How do you imagine that?

Re-read the words in chapter 21. What aspects of the Trinity – Father, Son, and Holy Spirit – do you discern in this passage? Given your studies these past several weeks, what new understanding / insight do you have about the three-in-one nature of our Lord? Discuss.

Today, I am grateful to God for

1.

2.

3.

*4.

*5.

Today, I served / plan to serve

Today, I worshiped the Holy Spirit through this music

Breath Prayer

Holy Spirit, abide in me and make me yours, I pray…

Holy Spirit, breathe in me and bring me life in You.

Day 21 Habit-Check

Go back over your homework for the past three weeks. Look at your answers to questions, your gratitude lists, and your acts of service. Make a list of the three most impactful take-aways from your work:

1.

2.

3.

Reflect: What made those three things impactful to you?

How might God be communicating to you, through those impactful things, about His desire for your next steps?

Write a prayer to God – Father, Son, and Holy Spirit. Praise God for His perfect character and steadfast faithfulness. Thank God for His rescue, forgiveness, and love. And ask God for His anointing and empowerment as you persist beyond the 21-day mark in this study, building holy habits for the new beginning God has in mind!

Place of Prayer

Do not remember the former things,
  or consider the things of old.
I am about to do a new thing;
  now it springs forth, do you not perceive it?
I will make a way in the wilderness
  and rivers in the desert. —Isaiah 43:18 - 19

Week Four

Where We've Been: Past

As we mark our "Habit Milestone" of 21 days in this study, we apply what we know about our identities as God's children to what we have known about our identities as people in the world. Where are the hurts that need healing? Where are the lies that need correcting? The past does not define us.

Defanging the Past

Having established our 21-day habit of prayer, scripture study, and faith-in-action, we are going to build on that pattern as we shift our focus a bit. For the last 3 weeks, we have reviewed who God is and considered what that means about our own identities as creations of God, made in God's image, members of God's Body and family.

Holding onto the truths we've articulated, we are going to go deeper now – to excavate details about who each of us is, individually, at this point in time – as specific people, unique, with one-of-a-kind histories.

Why is this kind of introspection important? Because God's influence is not the only influence that shapes us. Each of us has seen, heard, and experienced a vast number of ideas that have either amplified or undermined the truths of God and our identity in God. Naming and understanding those influences mitigates their power over us.

Just how powerful can such influences be? Consider this example:

Gilda Radner, American comedienne extraordinaire, told an amazing story about a dog she owned as a child. This dog, Lucy, was hit by a car while pregnant with puppies. Lucy survived, but her two back legs had to be amputated. She adapted quite quickly, teaching herself to get around by dragging herself on her front legs. All went well with her puppies' births, and Lucy was a good mama – feeding the pups and caring for them so they flourished. But imagine the surprise of Gilda and her family when they realized that Lucy's pups – all of whom had four healthy legs – were learning to get around by dragging themselves on their front legs. Just like their mama.

This story has so much truth in it. We are shaped by the world around us from the time we are born, and sometimes those who love us most cripple us without meaning to. We can go through our entire lifetimes, dragging someone else's infirmity as our own.

Painful Past, Still Present

I can trace my own craving for fresh starts to the chaos of my childhood home. The first day of school always thrilled me because it seemed to offer an orderly, predictable, safe alternative. I cherished all the accoutrements: freshly sharpened, rubber-scented pencils; notebooks pristine and empty; new shoes shiny… those little things hinted to me that here, I would be secure. Here, there would be order. Because of those associations, the first day of school was always a magical day for me, and school itself was both my reprieve and rescue.

But when my father's Air Force career was cut short in the middle of my 6th grade year, that first day of school sweetness was just one of the myriad casualties. We returned to the U.S.A. from a long-time duty station in the Netherlands. Everything familiar disappeared, except for the volatility that came with us wherever we went. Staying with my grandparents while my father searched for a new vocational path, I had to start at a new school mid-year. That first day of school wasn't a "real" first day. It was an interruption of someone else's well-established routine. I hated every minute.

As the emphatic outsider – scared, resentful, alienated – I resisted this fresh start with all my adolescent energy. Sitting alone in the vast, cacophonous cafeteria, I had a powerful lesson in "being alone in a crowd." Feeling homeless and friendless exacerbated my sense of hopelessness. This "new beginning" was unwelcome and unwelcoming – all I wanted to do was go back to the way things had been before

So many choices in my life can be traced back to that miserable day as a desolate eleven-year-old! My defense mechanisms, my determination to appear strong, my resistance to grieving – so much of middle-aged me connects directly to that broken little girl.

What about you? Where in your past are the origins of your present? And are they helping you – or harassing you relentlessly?

Face Forward

A pastor pal of mine likes to point out that rearview mirrors are a fraction the size of windshields. On purpose. What's ahead, she maintains, is what matters – both when we're driving and when we're following God. Staying on track requires the occasional backward glance, but an inordinate focus on what's behind us will land us in the ditch literally and metaphorically.

So, this week we will work on identifying and disentangling from anything in our past that is distracting us from our present.

Habits of the Heart

As in the first 3 weeks of our study, there will be daily prayers and daily scripture passages and questions. We will continue with daily gratitude lists – 5 thanks offerings, your choice. We will also incorporate a specific daily challenge / action item.

Why are we upping the ante of action to the mix?

Because Jesus was a man action who insisted on His followers becoming like Him.

"Now that you know these things, you are blessed *if you do them*," Jesus told His disciples. (John 13:17, emphasis added)

The disciple John, encouraged the early church, "Little children, let us love, not in word or speech, but in truth and action." (1 John 3:18)

And James, the brother of Jesus, spelled it out for his congregation in Jerusalem: "Be doers of the word and not merely hearers… those who look into the perfect law, the law of liberty, and persevere, being not hearers who forget but doers who act—*they will be blessed in their doing*." (James 1:22 & 25, emphasis added)

These words about active application of truth connect back to an early teaching of Jesus and reflect the way Jesus saw "witness" as more than words. When asked what the first commandment was, Jesus responded: "You shall love the Lord your God with all your heart, soul, mind, and strength. And you shall love your neighbor as yourself." (Mark 12:30 – 31) Love of God, love of neighbor. Jesus's stated priorities were clearly Jesus's walked-out / lived-out priorities, too.

As we pray and study scripture, we continue to make a holy habit of actively loving God daily. Incorporating daily actions helps us make a holy habit of loving our neighbor. So, please lean into this added element, and enjoy knowing that your devotion is a direct response to Jesus and makes you look a lot like Him!

Where We've Been: The Past

Week Four Prayers

Adapted from Psalm 139: 1 – 18

O Lord, You have searched me and known me.
You know when I sit down and when I rise up;
    You discern my thoughts from far away.
Even before a word is on my tongue, O Lord, you know it completely.

Where can I go from Your spirit?
    Or where can I flee from Your presence?
If I ascend to heaven, You are there;
    if I make my bed in shadowy places, You are there.
If I take the wings of the morning
    and settle at the farthest limits of the sea,
even there Your hand shall lead me; You shall hold me fast.
The darkness cannot hide me from You, Lord.

I am fearfully and wonderfully made, because all Your works are good.
  How weighty to me are Your thoughts, O God!
    How vast is the sum of them!
I try to count them—they are more than the sand;
    I come to the end—I am still with You.

Breath Prayer Version

Inhale: You know me through and through, Lord God.

Exhale: Hold me; heal me; make me whole, Lord God.

WEEK FOUR ACTION ITEMS

View this week's introduction video at shannonvowell.com.

Daily tasks specified each day.

Gratitude List each day – five offerings of thanks, your choice.

As you prepare for this week's study, please think about the following questions:

1. How many of the hurts, heartaches, and bad habits of my present have specific roots in my past?

2. How do I tend to cope with past trauma? Do I tend to forget about it? Deny its impact? Work through it with professional help? Some other tactic? A combination? Discuss.

Day 1

READ 1 Samuel 16:4 – 11; Judges 6:1 – 15

Based on this reading, how did Jesse see his youngest son, David?

Based on Gideon's words, what was his status in his father's household?

How are David and Gideon similar in these accounts?

How did your parents see you / what was your status in your family of origin? How do you know?

What words from your father most impacted you?

What words from your mother most impacted you?

Other thoughts on this?

ACTION ITEM

If your "impact words" were positive, thank your parent(s) for them. If they were negative, find someone whom you can encourage with words that you would have liked to hear as a child.

Today, I am grateful to God for

1.
2.
3.
4.
5.

> ***Breath Prayer***
>
> You know me through and through, Lord God.
>
> Hold me; heal me; make me whole, Lord God.

Day 2

READ Judges 6:1 – 15; John 4:5 – 25

How did Gideon's family circumstances, socioeconomic status, and nationality affect his self-image?

How did the Samaritan woman's circumstances, socioeconomic status, and nationality affect her self-image?

Recall your own childhood understanding of circumstances, socioeconomic status, and nationality. Describe them.

How did these factors inform your understanding of your identity and your place and purpose in the world?

How has your understanding of your identity and your place and purpose in the world changed during adulthood?

ACTION ITEM

Research where hungry people can go in your area for food assistance. Make a donation to the feeding ministry of your choice.

Today, I am grateful to God for

1.
2.
3.
4.
5.

> **Breath Prayer**
>
> You know me through and through, Lord God.
>
> Hold me; heal me; make me whole, Lord God.

Day 3

READ 1 Kings 12:20 – 30; 1 Kings 14:7 – 16

What turning point do you see in Jeroboam's life?

What was the catalyst / who was the motivation?

What was the outcome?

What big turning points have there been in your life?

What catalyzed them / who motivated them?

What were the outcomes?

Do you regret any of these turning points?

If you do, have you forgiven yourself / others?

ACTION ITEM

Read "The Necklace" by Guy de Maupassant (available on multiple sites online). How does this story illustrate the dangers of unexamined / misunderstood turning points?

Today, I am grateful to God for

1.
2.
3.
4.
5.

> ***Breath Prayer***
>
> You know me through and through, Lord God.
>
> Hold me; heal me; make me whole, Lord God.

Day 4

READ   Judges 6:11 – 16, & 7:15 – 23 Ruth 1:1 – 22, & 4:13 – 17

Summarize Gideon's initial self-assessment.

How was it proved wrong?

Summarize Naomi's initial assessment of Ruth.

How was it proved wrong?

Have you ever experienced similar correctives to your own self-assessment? Describe.

Have you ever experienced similar correctives to the assessments other people have made of you? Describe.

ACTION ITEM

Write on a piece of paper three of the most poisonous labels, comments, or denigrations that have been targeted at you – by others or by yourself. Take the paper outside, put it into a metal bowl, and burn it. Write the words "Chosen by God; Cherished by God" on a clean sheet of paper and tape it where you will see it every day.

Today, I am grateful to God for

1.
2.
3.
4.
5.

> **Breath Prayer**
>
> You know me through and through, Lord God.
>
> Hold me; heal me; make me whole, Lord God.

Day 5

READ   Psalm 23; Psalm 51; 2 Corinthians 5:17

Reflect on the fact that both Psalms were written by King David (the youngest son overlooked by his father in our first day's reading, and the grandson of Ruth's son Obed). How are the Psalms different?

What does it mean to you that someone who penned Psalm 23 is the author of the most influential confession and plea for forgiveness in Christian history? Specifically, what does that imply about beginning... again ... with God?

How do these Psalms apply to your own history?

Look back over your notes from this week, and then re-read the 2 Corinthians verse. How does the newness of Christ impact what you know about your past / your self?

ACTION ITEM

Apologize to someone you have hurt. Apologize to yourself for self-inflicted wounds. Confess present sins to the Lord. Then write out 2 Corinthians 5:17 on five different sticky notes and place them where you will be reminded: you are forgiven and made new!

Today, I am grateful to God for

1.
2.
3.
4.
5.

> **Breath Prayer**
>
> You know me through and through, Lord God.
>
> Hold me; heal me; make me whole, Lord God.

The Still Place

*This one thing I do: forgetting what lies behind and straining forward to what lies ahead,
I press on toward the goal for the prize of the heavenly call of God in Christ Jesus.*

—Philippians 3:13b - 14

Week Five

Where We Are: Present I

Assessing our present state requires a long look in the mirror – of our souls! Are we who we say we are? Are we who we want to be? Where are we succeeding and where do we need help? God delights in our deliverance.

Invited by God, to "the Present!"

Last week we spent time exploring ways that people and events in our past have shaped our understanding of ourselves, life, and God.

This week we will seek to see ourselves, life, and God in light of the truth of this moment, right now. The shift in focus is not because the past doesn't matter, but *because the past is not our master.*

Our God is a God of "new morning mercies," who "makes all things new," and is ever "doing a new thing" (Lamentations 3:23, Revelation 21:5, Isaiah 3:22 – 23). Because of Who God is, today is not bound by the bonds of yesterday!

We've already spent some time studying God's authority and the ways it blesses us, generally. Now we'll look for the ways that God's authority intersects with our moment-by-moment right-now lives. God's invitation into the newness of today can only happen because God has the authority over us, and newness, and today.

Invitations and Authority

There are no earthly parallels to God's authority, of course, but earthly comparisons can clarify just how much God's invitation means to us.

For example, some years ago when I was a graduate student at Cambridge University, two experiences taught me the incomparable benefit of "being invited" by highly-placed friends.

1. My favorite living novelist – Margaret Atwood – was visiting campus and giving a lecture. I was SO excited! When I shared my enthusiasm with a friend who was a Fellow of my residential college, she promptly invited me to an event that hadn't been publicized because it was so "select," a Fellows Luncheon with Atwood. There was a HUGE difference between sitting in a packed lecture hall to hear Atwood speak from a podium vs. sitting next to her while we both ate soup and she answered questions. I was only included in the latter because of my friend. "Being invited" = being brought into an intimate circle with a living legend.

2. Similarly, the director of my interdisciplinary academic program at Cambridge took me under wing and invited me to a dinner of University Fellows – an event not only not publicized or open to the public, but actually *secret*. I got to be a wide-eyed participant in a meal that was marked by rituals dating back to the 1100s (including taking snuff from the horn of a now-extinct ruminant). Our meal was served by candlelight in a hall built in the 16th century, and was accompanied by wines and ports the like of which I will never partake again in this lifetime. I felt as though I had somehow stepped into a magic, medieval realm for one evening's unforgettable feast. My friend's influence and authority conferred privileges and pleasures on me that I will never forget. "Being invited" = being brought into an old and ongoing tradition of elaborate remembrance and celebration.

Note that neither of these experiences would have been mine if I had not been invited by "insiders."

And note that neither of these experiences would have been mine if I had declined their invitations.

In both respects, these experiences demonstrate the both / and of Jesus's invitation to us in the present moment.

The amazing gift of the present is ours only because Jesus offers it to us; and we can only experience the "amazing" Jesus is offering if we accept His invitation.

Interestingly, both the thrill of my first example – rubbing elbows with a living legend – and the marvel of my second example – being included in extremely privileged traditions and pleasures – are thrills that mimic (in a muted, limited, earth-bound way) the thrills Jesus offers us in the present moment. Jesus's invitation is to rub elbows – with Him! Jesus's invitation is to feast – at the supper of the Lamb! There is nothing and no one more thrilling than what and who He offers!

So... the work this week aims to give us eyes to see and ears to hear that invitation from Jesus – and to give us excited hearts and lips that we might answer, "Yes, please!"

> Let us then approach God's throne of grace with confidence, so that we may receive mercy and find grace to help us in our time of need. *–Hebrews 4:16*

A Few Changes this Week

A new feature in your daily work – the "starting point" question. Before you read your scripture verses, you'll be asked to respond to a question that will give you insight into your own perspectives and preconceptions. Please answer candidly – there are no "wrong" answers.

A new organizational feature in your daily reading – "clusters" of scripture. Most days this week will assign scripture reading in small groups, or clusters. It may be helpful to answer questions as you complete the reading for each cluster. Or, if you prefer to read straight through all the assigned scriptures up front, be prepared to go back and review each cluster in light of the questions asked about it.

Where We Are: Present I

Week Five Prayers

Adapted from Paul's letter to the Ephesians 1:3 – 8

Lord God, Father, Son, and Holy Spirit, blessed are You today!

And Lord God, Father, Son, and Holy Spirit, blessed am *I* today – because I am *Your*s!

You have blessed me, Lord, with every spiritual blessing in the heavenly places.

You chose me, Father, before the foundation of the world, to be holy and blameless before You in love. You destined me, Father, for adoption as Your child! I am Yours, Father, according to Your own good pleasure. I am Yours!

In You, Lord Jesus, I have redemption. In You, Lord Jesus, I have the forgiveness of my trespasses. In You, Lord Jesus, I have the riches of Your lavish grace.

Holy Spirit, abide in me this day, that my life might proclaim Your glory. I am a living temple for You. I surrender joyfully to Your purposes!

Amen.

Breath Prayer Version

Inhale: Father, Son, Holy Spirit – invite me into Yourself today

Exhale: Father, Son, Holy Spirit – I say "yes" to you today

WEEK FIVE ACTION ITEMS

View this week's introduction video at shannonvowell.com.

A "starting point" question, to identify personal perspective.

Daily tasks specified each day.

Gratitude List each day – five offerings of thanks, your choice.

Before you prepare for this week's work, think about the following questions:

1. Where in your life right now do you feel God's pleasure and presence most strongly? In what activities, relationships, and habits of thought and action are you most peacefully confident of being obedient to God?

2. Where in your life right now do you feel stuck / sad / distant from the Lord? In what activities, relationships, and habits of thought and action are you least peacefully confident of being obedient to God?

Day 1

STARTING POINT What makes you valuable, right now, today? Common measures of self-value include family connection, education, professional competency / prestige, wealth… In your assessment, how valuable are you, and why?

READ the following sets of verses.
   Cluster 1: Exodus 28:1 & Leviticus 10:1 – 3;
   Cluster 2: Matthew 18:1 – 5 & 12 – 13;
   Cluster 3: Philippians 3:3 – 9

Cluster 1: What might Nadab, Abihu, and Aaron have assumed about their privileged status conferring an extra measure of protection from God's wrath? How do the verses in cluster 1 correct those assumptions?

Do you ever make assumptions about your own privilege – or lack of privilege – based on your parents / family line? Your education? Your citizenship? Something else?

Cluster 2: What do Jesus's words about children indicate? Who are "the 99"? What does that mean to you?

Cluster 3: Paul's words to the Philippians describe all Paul's worldly claims to value – heritage, education, zealous religious practice, etc. But what does Paul say about the value of those things? Do you agree with him? Why / why not?

Based solely on what you've read today, what makes you valuable?

Compare this last response to your response to the Starting Point question.

ACTION ITEM

Watch the movie "Mary and Martha" (Hillary Swank, 2013). What kinds of "personal value" issues does this movie raise? How / does it contribute to your understanding of your own value?

Today, I am grateful to God for

1.
2.
3.
4.
5.

> *Breath Prayer*
>
> Father, Son, Holy Spirit –
> invite me into Yourself today
>
> Father, Son, Holy Spirit –
> I say "yes" to you today

Day 2

STARTING POINT What makes you attractive, right now, today?

READ the following sets of verses.
   Cluster 1: 2 Samuel 14:25 – 26; 15:5 – 6; Matthew 7:15 – 20
   Cluster 2: Proverbs 11:22; 1 Peter 3:3 – 4; 1 Timothy 2:8 – 10;
   2 Corinthians 2:14 - 16

Cluster 1: How do these scriptures relate to each other? (Think in terms of Absalom's gorgeousness & wickedness.)

Have you ever known someone whose character and appearance were completely at odds? Describe.

Cluster 2: How do these scriptures relate to each other? (Think in terms of feminine beauty and magnetism.)

In our culture, how much traction do ideas like the ones in the cluster 2 verses get? Analyze possible reasons for this disparity.

Based on these scripture verses, what constitutes an "attractive" person? Be as thorough as possible, citing elements from all three clusters!

Using the rubric you just articulated, evaluate your own attractiveness below.

Compare what you just wrote with your response to the Starting Point question.

ACTION ITEM

Write a card or letter to someone who is truly beautiful by scripture's standards. Thank him / her for having the "aroma of Christ" and name several ways he / she embodies Jesus to you.

Today, I am grateful to God for

1.
2.
3.
4.
5.

> *Breath Prayer*
>
> Father, Son, Holy Spirit –
> invite me into Yourself today
>
> Father, Son, Holy Spirit –
> I say "yes" to you today

Day 3

STARTING POINT Are you authentic? How do you know?

READ the following sets of verses.
   Cluster 1: 1 Kings 18:21 – 39; Acts 8:9 – 24; Acts 19:11 – 16
   Cluster 2: Luke 19:1 – 10; Acts 4:36 – 5:11

Cluster 1: What is authentic about the prophets of Baal? Why do they fail? What is authentic about Simon? What gets him in trouble? What (if anything) is authentic about the sons of Sceva?

What do the efforts of all these men cost them?

Cluster 2: What parallels do you see between the story of Zacchaeus and the events with Barnabas, Ananias, and Sapphira in the early church? Consider, for example, the ways in which Barnabas and Zacchaeus are alike in motive and action.

What points of contrast do you see?

Thinking about authenticity – if Zacchaeus had said all the things he said in response to Jesus, and then not followed through on his promises, what do you think would have been the result?

ACTION ITEM

Bake a batch of cookies or make bread – from scratch. Invite family or friends to share in what you make. Ask them to describe the "authentic" taste of home-made food.

Today, I am grateful to God for

1.
2.
3.
4.
5.

> **Breath Prayer**
>
> Father, Son, Holy Spirit –
> invite me into Yourself today
>
> Father, Son, Holy Spirit –
> I say "yes" to you today

Day 4

STARTING POINT In your opinion, how much are action and authenticity connected? Explain.

READ the following sets of verses.
  Cluster 1: Isaiah 29:11 – 16; Ezekiel 33:31 – 32; Matthew 15:6 – 9
  Cluster 2: Matthew 7:21; Matthew 21:28 – 32; Matthew 25:31 – 46

Cluster 1: Paraphrase the theme of these passages. What is God's observation about His people? What is the implicit warning?

Think about your experience of Christian worship and community. Have you encountered situations like the ones described in these verses? How did it make you feel? What did you do in response?

Cluster 2: What is Jesus saying about actions here? According to Jesus, how are actions a requirement for authentic Christian living?

Does this have any bearing on your own walk / witness? Explain.

Based on the passages you've studied today, what does it mean to be scripturally authentic? Write a definition below.

Compare your definition above to your answer to the Starting Point question for yesterday.

ACTION ITEM

Do a little research on "authenticity" in an area of interest to you. For example, why is the word "champagne" strictly limited and licensed? Or, what's the critical distinction between diamonds and lookalike cubic zirconia? Or, what is the training process for recognizing counterfeit money? See how much of what you learn applies to your Christian authenticity.

Today, I am grateful to God for

1.
2.
3.
4.
5.

> ***Breath Prayer***
>
> Father, Son, Holy Spirit –
> invite me into Yourself today
>
> Father, Son, Holy Spirit –
> I say "yes" to you today

Day 5

STARTING POINT What situation in your life right now looks the most "impossible"?

READ   Luke 7:11 – 15; Acts 9:36 – 41; John 11:1 – 15; 35 – 44

In these passages, various people are raised from the dead. Name the people who were raised and name the people who did the raising.

In your opinion, why were these people raised?

Lazarus was one of Jesus's closest friends. But what do the other stories imply about God's love for the anonymous widow mother at Nain and the nameless widows of Joppa? Discuss.

What do today's readings have to say to your "impossible" circumstances?

ACTION ITEM

Do something concrete to serve someone in an "impossible" situation. Some ideas: Bring balloons to a children's cancer ward. Work a shift at your local food bank. Volunteer for an adult literacy program. Pack a shoebox for Operation Christmas Child.

Today, I am grateful to God for

1.
2.
3.
4.
5.

> **Breath Prayer**
>
> Father, Son, Holy Spirit –
> invite me into Yourself today
>
> Father, Son, Holy Spirit –
> I say "yes" to you today

Day 35 Habit-Check

Go back over your homework for the past two weeks. Look at your answers to questions, your gratitude lists, and your acts of service. Make a list of the three most impactful take-aways from your work:

1.

2.

3.

Reflect: What made those three things impactful to you?

How might God be communicating to you, through those impactful things, about His desire for your next steps?

Based on the last two weeks work, what are you learning about yourself?

Waiting for the Day

This is the day that the Lord has made;
let us rejoice and be glad in it.

—Psalm 118:24

Week Six

Where We Are: Present II

We continue, this week, working to get our arms around the real-life truth of right now. We know this reality is fluid and fragile. We seek the firm foundation of Christ to stabilize all that needs to stay put; we submit to the searching of the Spirit to help us discern all that needs to be set aside, healed, or transformed.

Receiving the Gift of the Present

I was an adult when I heard this hard-punching little poem:
>*Yesterday is history.*
>*Tomorrow is a mystery.*
>*But today is a gift; that's why they call it "the present."*

I love the way those three short lines spell out the cosmic truth of time: all we have is RIGHT NOW.

As we explored in Week 4, the past can be more than history. The past can be a boat anchor. The past can be a locked prison cell. The past can be a suffocating, oppressive fog of guilt and regret. One thing the past cannot be: changed.

The future is similarly out of our reach and immune to our efforts to control – as anyone who has ever had to "change plans" can attest.

But today... this very moment... that's the place in time where we actually live, and in which we are called to glorify God. Not yesterday or last year or when we were young – not tomorrow or someday or when we are old – today. Now. This is the holy moment; there can be no other.

"Receive" is an Active Verb

Receiving the gift of the present requires something of us. God offers us the gift – but we can receive or refuse it. A choice is required – an action – either way.

Even if we choose to receive the gift, our choice begins the process, but it doesn't end it. Think of receiving a wrapped package from someone on your birthday. If you take the package into your hands, say "thank you," and then set the package aside, have you really received the gift? Of course not. The package must be opened. Its contents must be seen and understood and used appropriately. Receiving is a multi-step, active assent to the Giver!

Fully receiving requires discernment, too. Think of the potential disasters if a gift is received but then used improperly: a bicycle used as a piece of jewelry, or a book used as a cooking implement!

Receiving a gift requires acknowledging the specific nature of the gift and enjoying it in a way appropriate to its nature.

God's good gifts always come to us with purpose and power; we always have multiple options in response, including refusal or misuse. Receiving God's gifts requires us to be responsible!

Receiving the Gift = Influencing the Outcome

Our multi-faceted responsibility to the gift of the present comes with an exponential potential in the form of our influence. A favorite book of scripture which speaks directly to the power of influence is the book of Esther. Esther's story illustrates how God employs his faithful people to address contemporary issues – to bring God's eternal truth to life in the right now.

Improbably elevated to be Queen of Persia, Jewish orphan Esther finds herself suddenly swept up in a plot hatched by the evil Hamon – a plot to wipe out the whole Jewish race! The secret of Esther's identity, the unpredictable affections of the King, and harsh laws governing access to the King create excruciating stress as Esther's uncle Mordecai insists she use her influence.

Having received God's gifts of power and privilege, Mordecai implies, Esther must now leverage those gifts for God's purposes in the present moment. "It is for such a time as this," he tells Esther, "that you have come to royal dignity." (Esther 4:14)

We are probably not resident in palaces or poised to avert genocides, but our positions and our circumstances are no less powerfully purposed than Esther's – and part of our personal reception of the gift of the present is our willingness to be used by God, right where we are.

Like Esther, our influence in our homes, places of work, and communities is unique. Like Esther, our opportunities to exert that influence are urgently important – it's not just ourselves we are impacting! And like Esther, the impact of our influence rests in the timeliness of our response to God.

We are full circle: the gift God gives is right now.

> But encourage one another every day,
> as long as it is called "today"... –*Hebrews 13a*

As we head into a second week of focusing ourselves on the movement of God in the present moment, let's keep both the "invitational" and the "offered gift" aspect of this window in time fully in view. Jesus is doing the inviting. Jesus is doing the offering. Our part is to say "yes!" and show up. Our part is to say "thank you," open the package, and get on with using and enjoying the gift even as we share it with others. Our part is to acknowledge our influence and then make it available to God.

Blessedly, as we have already learned, "our part" is powered by the Holy Spirit within us.

Where We Are: The Present II

Week Six Prayers

Adapted from Paul's letter to the Ephesians 1:3 – 8

Lord God, Father, Son, and Holy Spirit, blessed are You today!

And Lord God, Father, Son, and Holy Spirit, blessed am *I* today – because I am *Your*s!

You have blessed me, Lord, with every spiritual blessing in the heavenly places.

You chose me, Father, before the foundation of the world, to be holy and blameless before You in love. You destined me, Father, for adoption as Your child! I am Yours, Father, according to Your own good pleasure. I am Yours!

In You, Lord Jesus, I have redemption. In You, Lord Jesus, I have the forgiveness of my trespasses. In You, Lord Jesus, I have the riches of Your lavish grace.

Holy Spirit, abide in me this day, that my life might proclaim Your glory. I am a living temple for You. I surrender joyfully to Your purposes!

Amen.

Breath Prayer Version

Inhale: Father, Son, Holy Spirit, I offer you the gift of my life today

Exhale: Father, Son, Holy Spirit, I receive the gift of Your love today

WEEK SIX ACTION ITEMS

View this week's introduction video at shannonvowell.com.

A "starting point" question, to identify personal perspective.

Daily tasks specified each day.

Gratitude List each day – five offerings of thanks, your choice.

Before you begin this week's work, think about the following questions:

1. Have you ever given a present that turned up later in a "re-gifting" situation? Was there a gift you did not receive, at any point in your life, that still makes you sad to recall? How do such experiences influence your receptivity to Jesus's gift to you of the present moment?

2. Think about the connection between being invited and feeling included. How do your experiences with invitations / inclusion / being left out impact you as you consider Jesus's invitation to you to live for and with Him, today?

Day 1

STARTING POINT Many Christians who acknowledge that they are valuable because Jesus loves them maintain they are unimportant to Jesus's plan for the world. Lack of obvious / public gifts, lack of money, lack of physical strength, lack in general are common explanations for individual unimportance. What about you? Do you think you are important to Jesus's plan for the world? Why / why not?

READ the following sets of verses.
   Cluster 1:   Exodus 36:1 – 7; Acts 18:1 – 4; 24 – 28
   Cluster 2:   Luke 8:1 – 3; Acts 6:1 – 6

Cluster 1: Here, we encounter two different groups of workers. First, craftspeople who are given the task of creating the Tabernacle for worship of God. Second, tentmakers who become temporary partners with Paul. Based on these passages, what kinds of inferences can you make about the importance of work – whether it's directly for God (as in the Temple craftspeople) or not (as in tent-making)?

Describe the way Priscilla and Aquilla become Christian mentors "accidentally."

Connect that "accident" with modern ideas about networking and brainstorm ways that work can be important to Jesus's Kingdom, even indirectly.

Cluster 2: Two different groups of ministry supporters are described here. Who are they, and what do they do? How are their efforts important? Are either / both of those kinds of support still going on in the present-day church? Are they important now? Explain.

Review the people and activities we've analyzed in today's readings. Where do you see yourself in these scriptures? With whom do you identify, and why?

Glance back at your notes from Day 1 of last week. Based on what you read and wrote then and today, re-evaluate your understanding of your own value and importance. New insights?

ACTION ITEM

Who has been important to your faith journey – and doesn't know it? Call, text, or email that person and let him / her know why their work or witness matters greatly to you and to Jesus's plan for the world!

Today, I am grateful to God for

1.
2.
3.
4.
5.

> **Breath Prayer**
>
> Father, Son, Holy Spirit, I offer you the gift of my life today
>
> Father, Son, Holy Spirit, I receive the gift of Your love today

Day 2

STARTING POINT How would you describe your present state of mind? To what extent is your state of mind a result of "big-picture" things like political conflict, global health crises, natural disasters, etc.?

READ
   Cluster 1: Proverbs 18:10; Psalm 91; Psalm 119:90; Romans 8:31 – 39
   Cluster 2: Matthew 6:25 – 34; Habakkuk 3:17 - 19

Cluster 1: What claims do these verses make? List them below.

If these claims are true, what is the truth of your present level of safety, security, and belovedness?

If the truth you just articulated above is based in God's character and not in any circumstances, how logical is anxiety? Explain.

Cluster 2: These verses are more instructional than explanatory. What instructions do they give?

In what way do these instructions rely on the logic of / the truth articulated in the verses in cluster 1? Explain.

ACTION ITEM Memorize Isaiah 26:3 –

*"Those of steadfast mind You keep in peace,
In peace because they trust in You."*

Today, I am grateful to God for

1.
2.
3.
4.
5.

Breath Prayer

Father, Son, Holy Spirit, I offer you the gift of my life today

Father, Son, Holy Spirit, I receive the gift of Your love today

Day 3

STARTING POINT A dominant characteristic of our times is division. Words like "partisan," "extremist," "conspiracy theory,", "polarization," etc., are commonplace in our conversations about world events. How does this aspect of our present reality intersect with your Christian worldview? Explain in as much detail as possible below:

READ the following sets of verses.
   Cluster 1: Matthew 10:16 – 39; 2 Corinthians 6:14 – 18
   Cluster 2: Psalm 16; Revelations 3:15 – 19
   Cluster 3: Romans 12:14 – 20

Cluster 1: Summarize the main points of these verses.

How comfortable are you with those ideas?

Cluster 2: Consider how these verses amplify the main points already articulated. What do they add?

Given all that we've read today, what do you think Paul means when he says "as much as it is up to you, be at peace with all people"?

ACTION ITEM

Do something kind / generous for someone with whom you vehemently disagree.

Today, I am grateful to God for

1.
2.
3.
4.
5.

> **Breath Prayer**
>
> Father, Son, Holy Spirit, I offer you the gift of my life today
>
> Father, Son, Holy Spirit, I receive the gift of Your love today

Day 4

STARTING POINT In what ways does your life illustrate your faith to a watching world? Be as specific as possible.

READ the following sets of verses.
   Cluster 1: John 13:1 – 17 & 35; 1 John 3:11 – 18
   Cluster 2: James 1:22 – 27; Luke 14:12 – 14

Cluster 1: Summarize what these verses have to say about living as a Christian.

John, who wrote both the scriptures in cluster one (John's gospel and the letters of John), referred to himself as "the disciple Jesus loved." Given the emphases just in the verses you read today, what do you make of that?

Cluster 2: The author of the book of James was Jesus's brother, who only came to faith after Jesus's resurrection. Knowing this, brainstorm ideas about the basis for James's instructions and priorities in this passage.

What do these scripture passages have to say to the idea that receiving God's gift of the present requires us to make our influence available to God?

ACTION ITEM

Watch "Babette's Feast" (1987). Think about the ways that poverty, hospitality, and sacrifice feature in the movie. Is the group portrayed "Christian," in your opinion? Why / why not?

Today, I am grateful to God for

1.
2.
3.
4.
5.

Breath Prayer

Father, Son, Holy Spirit, I offer you the gift of my life today

Father, Son, Holy Spirit, I receive the gift of Your love today

Day 5

STARTING POINT Paul said that "the love of money is the root of all kinds of evil." Agree or disagree with that statement, and back up your opinion with logic and experience.

READ Matthew 6:19 – 20; Luke 12:15 – 21; Corinthians 8:1 – 9

Okay, so these verses are all about money. How does that make you feel?

Jesus talks about money more than any other topic except "the Kingdom of Heaven." How does that make you feel?

Based on what you've read (not how you feel), how important is money in Christian witness? Provide as much detail as possible.

Look back over today's verses and list specific instructions and descriptions that you see there:

Look at your own financial records for the last 6 months. Based purely on those records, would an outside observer know you were a Christian? Why / why not?

ACTION ITEM

Do one thing to serve the poor in love today as an act of worship. Make sure your worship costs you time, effort, and money.

Today, I am grateful to God for

1.
2.
3.
4.
5.

> **Breath Prayer**
>
> Father, Son, Holy Spirit, I offer you the gift of my life today
>
> Father, Son, Holy Spirit, I receive the gift of Your love today

Re-Assessing the Invitation / Gift of the Present

As we wrap up our two weeks deep-dive into the present, let's review key concepts. Using your notes from this week and last week, respond to the following prompts.

- In this present moment, here are ways that I am valuable and can be important to God's purposes:

- In this present moment, here are ways that I am authentic and can be attractive as I live out God's calling:

- In this present moment, here are some of the reasons I know I am absolutely safe – no matter what my surrounding circumstances are:

- In this present moment, here is why my financial resources belong to God and how I can demonstrate that:

Sunrise Over Galilee

*But you are a chosen race, a royal priesthood, a holy nation, a people for his own possession,
that you may proclaim the excellencies of him who called you out of darkness into his marvelous light.*

—1 Peter 2:9

Week Seven

Why We're Here: Purpose

Our study and our practice are showing us ever more clearly: it's not about us. We are not in charge. Only God reigns. But at the same time, we have a very important role to play! This week, we align our personal purpose with God's glorious purposes for us.

Living On Purpose

Consider these quotes on "purpose" by various celebrated individuals.

Ask yourself: Do I agree? Why / why not? Does this resonate with what I have experienced to be true?

> Winston Churchill: "It is not enough to have lived. We should be determined to live for something."
>
> Michel de Montagne: "The soul which has no fixed purpose in life is lost; to be everywhere is to be nowhere."
>
> Thomas Carlyle: "The person without a purpose is like a ship without a rudder."
>
> JFK: "Efforts and courage are not enough without purpose and direction."
>
> Charles Dickens: "The best way to lengthen our days is to walk steadily and with a purpose."

"Purpose," according to these worthy individuals, provides meaning to life while orienting life in a particular direction. Purpose motivates, organizes, and consolidates. They agree "purpose" is important to achievement; they agree "purpose" is self-evidently good.

But *is* it?

Can the wrong purpose be more dangerous and disorienting than no purpose?

Consider the legacies of these people who indisputably gave themselves to lives of purpose: Nero. Napoleon. Hitler. The purposes of conquest and power-consolidation were clear and consistent in their lives, but the fruit of their purposeful living was self-evidently *bad* – even *evil*.

Polluted purpose is not unique to the monsters of history. What about the purpose peddled by our consumer culture? Marketers from Madison Avenue declare the stakes of the game of life, as they see it: "Accumulate wealth and prestigious possessions, because the one with the most stuff *wins*!"

What about the purpose proclaimed by our celebrity culture? "Use whatever means necessary to look young forever, and act like an adolescent as long as possible... the most popular-pretty-party-people *win*!"

Such superficial, petty definitions of "winning" are not exactly evil *a la* Hitler, but they aren't redolent with virtue in the way our opening quotes lead us to believe "purpose" will be, either. People who live according to these purposes will inevitably find life hollow at the core, as any cursory examination of token examples will prove. The anxious, insecure, peace-less lives of billionaires and "beautiful people" are a cliché.

Given the dubious reliability of generic purpose to imbue life with nobility and goodness, what might Churchill, Montagne, Carlyle, Kennedy, and Dickens have been taking for granted in their statements about purpose as obviously noble and good?

Other voices help us hone in on the distinction between purpose in general and good purpose in particular:

> Helen Keller: "True happiness is not obtained through self-gratification, but through fidelity to a worthy purpose."
>
> Mother Teresa: "I am a little pencil in the hand of a writing God, who is sending a love letter to the world."
>
> Billy Graham: "God did not make men and women haphazardly, but with an infinite plan and purpose."

In these musings on purpose, we get to the nitty-gritty of what makes purpose good. Worthiness, not self-gratification; love sent from God to the world; humility and surrender to God's good plan... These statements declare the true substance and basis for life-worthy purpose.

Of course, not one of us is Helen Keller, Mother Teresa, or Billy Graham! But isn't it interesting that those lives of out-size, lasting impact were guided by such specifically *humble* purposes? What might that suggest to us, as we seek specifics about our individual purposes through our work in this study?

This week our scripture readings will help us see the big-picture of God's good purpose as played out in small-picture lives. We will examine the possible ways that God's good purpose can have its full effect in our own small-picture lives, through our own unique circumstances and gifts. And we will work our way toward a "purpose statement" for ourselves – rooted in God's universal truth but specific to each of us.

For we are God's handiwork, created in Christ Jesus to do good works, which God prepared in advance for us to do. –*Ephesians 2:10*

Why We're Here: Purpose

Week Seven Prayers

Adapted from Peter's first letter, chapters 1 & 2

Holy and blessed Father, in Your mercy You have given me a new birth into a living hope!

You are keeping my inheritance, unfading and perfect, in heaven!

You are protecting me, even now, while I live today in hope!

Lead me in Your purpose today, Lord. Prepare my mind for action and give me self-control.

Open my mouth to proclaim Your mighty acts, because You called me out of darkness and into Your marvelous light!

And empower me, Lord, to keep my eyes fixed on the goodness of Jesus Christ, no matter what this day may hold.

Amen.

Breath Prayer Version

Inhale: Lord, my purpose is to live in Your perfect Light and Love

Exhale: Lord, fulfill Your purpose in my life today, I pray

WEEK SEVEN ACTION ITEMS

View this week's introduction video at shannonvowell.com.

A "starting point" question, to identify personal perspective.

Daily tasks specified each day.

Gratitude List each day – five offerings of thanks, your choice.

Before you begin this week's work, think about the following questions:

1. Successful corporations craft "purpose statements" (also called "mission statements") in order to align their activities and endeavors. Look up a few of your favorite corporations and see whether their purpose statements ring true to you. What works? What doesn't? Why?

2. Taking into consideration what you've written above as well as the quotes we looked at in the introduction to this week's work, draft a few different purpose statements for yourself. Don't try to craft the perfect purpose statement just yet! Rather, try out different iterations... and have fun.

Day 1

STARTING POINT In your opinion, why are you, personally, here (alive / on earth / in this season)?

READ Psalm 139:1 – 18; Jeremiah 1:4 – 8; Galatians 1:13 – 24

What overlap do you see in these very different passages of scripture? Look carefully, and make notes below.

What is specifically implied in Psalm 139:15 – 16; Jeremiah 1:5; and Galatians 1:15?

Does this impact your answer to the Starting Point question? If so, how?

Summarize Paul's description of his conversion in the Galatians passage. Who catalyzes the change? How many people are instrumental? What do you think this means?

When you think about your present circumstances, to what extent do you see them as

- consequences of mistakes (your own or other peoples)?

- rewards for good choices (your own or other peoples)?

- consequences of larger forces / circumstances beyond your control?

- specific parts of God's plan for your life?

ACTION ITEM

Watch the film "The Queen of Katwe." (Disney, 2016) Whose purpose is fulfilled in this story? How? What were the critical decision points? How does it apply to your life?

Today, I am grateful to God for

1.
2.
3.
4.
5.

> **Breath Prayer**
>
> Lord, my purpose is to live in Your perfect Light and Love
>
> Lord, fulfill Your purpose in my life today, I pray

Day 2

STARTING POINT Brainstorm at least five things that you would change about yourself / your circumstances right this moment, if you had the power to do so:

What would be the result, if those changes happened? What would look / feel / be different? Describe the changes below:

READ John 9:1 – 38

Summarize this amazing story below, including all the characters mentioned:

Why were the Pharisees so resistant to accepting the miracle?

Why were the man's parents so resistant to testifying to the miracle? Any overlap with the Pharisees?

According to Jesus, what was the point of the miracle? (See verses 3 & 38)

Look back at your Starting Point list. Where can you apply the truths of this miracle of healing in your own places that need healing?

ACTION ITEM

Surrender your Starting Point list of change-items to God. Specifically, revisit the prayer for Week 3 and ask God to show you what is yours to change, what is His to change, and what is yours to surrender to Him.

Today, I am grateful to God for

1.
2.
3.
4.
5.

> **Breath Prayer**
>
> Lord, my purpose is to live in Your perfect Light and Love
>
> Lord, fulfill Your purpose in my life today, I pray

Day 3

STARTING POINT   How are you gifted, spiritually? List everything that comes to mind, below:

READ   1 Corinthians 12; Romans 12:1 – 8; Ephesians 4:1 – 16

List the spiritual gifts Paul identifies in these passages:

Can you think of other spiritual gifts – gifts from God that build up the whole of the Body (Christ's church)? If you can, list them below:

What does Paul have to say about the relative importance of the various spiritual gifts? Is this surprising to you? Why / why not?

What does Paul say is the purpose of spiritual gifts in the Corinthians passage?

What does he say is the purpose of spiritual gifts in the Ephesians passage?

In the Romans passage, what are the slightly different emphases Paul articulates?

Based on these passages, re-evaluate your spiritual gifts and draft a statement of purpose that applies to your use of them:

ACTION ITEM

Take a spiritual gifts inventory. The address below is one online assessment tool option.

www.ministrymatters.com/spiritualgifts

Today, I am grateful to God for

1.
2.
3.
4.
5.

> **Breath Prayer**
>
> Lord, my purpose is to live in Your perfect Light and Love
>
> Lord, fulfill Your purpose in my life today, I pray

Day 4

STARTING POINT What are your spheres of influence? Think in terms of personal, professional, and ministry connections. People you work and play alongside, people with whom you maintain long distance connections, etc. Brainstorm a list from those various spheres below:

READ Genesis 39:20 – 41:57; Esther 4:5 – 17; Nehemiah 1:1 – 2:8

Background: Joseph, favorite son of a wealthy Hebrew, had been sold into slavery by his jealous brothers. His master's wife had falsely accused him of rape prior to the passage you just read. What was Joseph's sphere of influence at the beginning of the passage? How did he use his influence? With whom did he share his gifts?

What was Joseph's sphere of influence at the end of the passage? How did his prison life directly lead to his being elevated?

Background: Esther, an orphan Jewess raised by her Uncle Mordecai, only became Queen because she won a beauty contest to replace the disgraced (rightful) Queen Vashti. What are Esther's spheres of influence in this passage? How does she operate within them? (If you don't know how the story ends, I encourage you to read the rest of the book of Esther – it's a thrilling conclusion!)

What are Nehemiah's spheres of influence? How do they overlap / intersect?

Think carefully about these characters. What do they have in common?

How much do their spheres of influence matter to their stories?

How much risk is involved for each, in these passages?

What do they accomplish – each of them / all of them – through their respective spheres of influence?

ACTION ITEM

Deliberately connect at least two people from different spheres of influence in your life. Strive to make Jesus the connecting point, and pray for God to use the new relationship to do something wonderful for His glory.

Today, I am grateful to God for

1.
2.
3.
4.
5.

> **Breath Prayer**
>
> Lord, my purpose is to live in Your perfect Light and Love
>
> Lord, fulfill Your purpose in my life today, I pray

Day 5

STARTING POINT Talk about your passions. What causes thrill your heart and motivate you to action? What do you LOVE to do? In what settings and activities do you feel most alive and close to God?

READ Psalm 16:11; Isaiah 64:8; Colossians 3:23 – 24; John 15:1 – 11

Summarize the main point of each of these passages:

- Psalm 16:11

- Isaiah 64:8

- Colossians 3:23 – 24

- John 15:1 – 11

Where do you see overlap? Explain.

Based on Jesus's concluding statement in the John passage, how much does "joy" figure in God's prescription for our working lives? What does that mean to you personally?

Based on what you wrote and read today, brainstorm possible applications for your next steps regarding your passions. Take into consideration what you've discovered about your spiritual gifts and your spheres of influence.

Look back at the potential Life Purpose statements you drafted at the beginning of this week. In the space below, write a new draft that incorporates what you've learned about yourself and God during these past few days.

ACTION ITEM

Do ONE concrete thing in pursuit of one of your passions / in support of one of your priorities. Write that step down below:

Today, I am grateful to God for

1.
2.
3.
4.
5.

> **Breath Prayer**
>
> Lord, my purpose is to live in Your perfect Light and Love
>
> Lord, fulfill Your purpose in my life today, I pray

Drawing Strength

Your word is a lamp to my feet and a light unto my path. — Psalm 119:105

*They are like trees
   planted by streams of water,
which yield their fruit in its season,
   and their leaves do not wither.
In all that they do, they prosper.* —Psalm 1:3

Week Eight

What's Next: Plan

Our new habits of prayer, Scripture study, and active servanthood will help us make a plan for the new beginning God has prepared for us. "Commit your work to the Lord, and your plans will be established." (Prov. 16:3) Amen!

Planning With Purpose

There is a famous saying: "Failing to plan is planning to fail."

Do you agree? Why / why not?

Our approach to planning can reveal a lot about the way we see ourselves and the world. Two of my dearest friends demonstrate how this plays out. One is addicted to "making plans." Her calendar must be *full* – travel, social engagements, classes, outings. When there is a blank space on the calendar, she feels anxious and diminished.

Conversely, the other is the opposite – she hates "making plans," preferring to preserve room for spontaneity and "being available" to God.

These women both lead busy, productive lives… but their attitudes toward planning reveal their hearts. For the first, "plans" equal security and value. For the second, preserving flexibility in her schedule for the Holy Spirit's leading connects her to the security and value she has in the Lord. Most of us fall somewhere between these two extremes, but our calendars still testify to our core beliefs.

Good Plans

Are there times when planning is essential, even as we look to God alone for our security and value? Most people would agree that building a house requires planning. There are literal "plans" that must be executed by an architect, approved by local authorities, and followed by the construction team. Each part of the building process requires advance planning – gathering supplies, contracting workers, coordinating with others. The order in which things occur is critical (electrical wires need to be in place before the dry wall installation – the concrete foundation should be poured before framing begins – etc.); that, too requires planning. Are there parallels in life, even the Christian life?

Interestingly, Jesus taught that being a Christian *required* a plan. In the gospel of Luke, Jesus explained to the crowds the costliness of following Him, and specified planning as a prerequisite for discipleship:

> For which of you, intending to build a tower, does not first sit down and estimate the cost, to see whether he has enough to complete it? Otherwise, when he has laid a foundation and is not able to finish, all who see it will begin to ridicule him, saying, 'This fellow began to build and was not able to finish.' (14:28 – 30)

This parable is followed immediately by a parable about a King setting out to do battle. If the King, while planning, pre-determines that he is not able to win, " ...then, while the other is still far away, he sends a delegation and asks for the terms of peace." (32)

Jesus, knowing that His own ability to "finish" was the cornerstone of God's plan to redeem the whole world, emphasized the gravity of planning not out of fear-mongering but out of love. Jesus wanted His beloved followers to be equipped to finish – equipped to follow Him to the very end – equipped to win the battle! So, He invited them (and us): Count the cost. Think it through.

God Plans

But here's where Jesus's version of planning is radically different from my friend's addictive calendar-filling: for Jesus, and for us in Jesus, the plan is *surrender*. Rather than planning in order to gain a sense of control over our days, Christians plan in humble obedience to God's control over our very lives. In that respect, my second friend's refusal to make too many plans is, itself, a form of planning. She is strategically preserving space for the Holy Spirit's use, trusting that her availability and God's leading will perfectly align.

This aspect of discipleship can be hard to embrace, especially if you have a longstanding habit of planning-to-the-nth-degree. But I'll share a story from my life that illustrates the way God is a better planner than we can ever hope to be.

I had a plan.

My life had taken a dramatic turn. I had planned to be married for a lifetime, but my first husband had changed his mind and left me to figure out an alternative. In the grief of seeing the first plan smashed to smithereens, I quickly turned to planning for therapy. And my new plan looked good to me. I would take two years to recover, grow my young sons up a bit, and then return to academic life in England – where we'd live much as we always had, just minus the husband.

With this plan in my hip pocket, I moved my children "temporarily" to the USA. Our two-year recovery period would segue quickly to a return to normal, I was sure.

God had a very (very!) different plan.

God's plan included meeting the love of my life, settling permanently in the States, and embarking on ministry as a vocation.

God's plan meant no more fancy degrees, but two precious daughters to enjoy! No international mobility, but a community to know and invest in over time. No "I did it my way" refrains in my ear, but ongoing "be thou my vision" as the background music for my days.

I thank God every day that His plan – not mine! – prevailed.

It can be terrifying to let go of the illusion of "control" that planning represents for many of us. We know we aren't really calling the shots, but our careful strategies and time management agendas allow us a façade of being In Charge. How to loosen our white-knuckle grasp of what is, ultimately, a mirage?

God's Good Plan

Jesus modelled the ultimate plan-as-surrender in the Garden of Gethsemane when He acknowledged God's plan and then asked for God's permission to opt out of it. His prayer there provides us with the perfect template for our plan-making in the here and now:

> Father, if You are willing, remove this cup from me; yet, **not my will but Yours be done**.
> –Luke 22:42 (emphasis added)

Based on Jesus's words and example, we can be confident that planning, for a Christian, requires ongoing flexibility and humility.

Called to imitate Christ, we should be ready to finish strong or ready to change course – ready to persevere or ready to pivot – ready to *follow*. Wherever and whenever God leads.

This week we are going to explore specific scriptural teaching on planning. Then we are going to apply that teaching to our identified spiritual gifts, our holy passions, and our individual purposes.

As we listen for God's voice, we will be consciously seeking a plan for our next steps in the journey with Him. By the end of this week's work, we will be marking 40 days of pilgrimage! That kind of investment of time and attention has holy consequences... and we will be praying for clarity and courage to take whatever next steps the Lord, in His goodness, leads us to take.

Praying for and with you.

What's Next: Plan

Week Eight Prayers

Adapted from Jeremiah 29:11, Proverbs 3:5 – 6, Proverbs 19:21, 2 Corinthians 10:5, Romans 8:28

Lord, You know the plans You have for me. You have good plans, Lord, plans to prosper me and not to harm me. Plans to give me a future. Plans to give me hope.

Lord, because You are so good and faithful, I trust You completely. I choose not to lean on my own understanding; I choose to lean into Your love and grace. I choose You, Lord – the Way! I choose the straight paths that You make for me!

Lord, I have plenty of ideas in my own mind, but it is Your plans that will stand and Your purposes that will prevail. So, Lord, I ask You to take every one of my thoughts captive to Your will.

And Lord, I ask You to make all things work together for my good and Your glory – today and forevermore. Amen

---

Breath Prayer Version (Psalm 143:8)

Inhale: Let me hear of Your steadfast love in the morning,
for in You I put my trust.

Exhale: Teach me the way I should go,
for to You I lift up my soul.

WEEK EIGHT ACTION ITEMS

View this week's introduction video at shannonvowell.com.

A "starting point" question, to identify personal perspective.

Daily tasks specified each day.

Gratitude List each day – five offerings of thanks, your choice.

Before you begin this week's work, think about the following questions:

- When I plan, do I lean toward – a control fetish? Self-distraction / self-soothing? People pleasing? Am I open to input? Am I closed? Attitudes I bring to planning:

- Do I ever plan based on my limitations? My expectations? My comfort? Describe.

- When my plans don't go as I had hoped, what's my tendency: to assign blame (to myself, to God, to others)? To chalk up another "failure"? To celebrate another "lesson"? Attitudes I bring to unplanned adjustments:

Day 1

STARTING POINT Does God have a big plan? If God does, where do you see yourself fitting into that plan?

READ John 6:22 – 40; Matthew 25:31 – 46

What does Jesus say is His job on earth?

What does Jesus say is our job on earth?

What connections do you see between the labors of love Jesus describes in the Matthew passage and the simple "believe" command in John?

Based on Jesus's teaching in John 6 and Matthew 25, brainstorm possibilities for your part in God's plan:

Compare / contrast what you wrote above with what you wrote in today's Starting Point.

ACTION ITEM

Identify five items in your house that have significant value (clothes, cooking pots and pans, furniture, etc.). Choose at least one of those items and make it "available" to God. Record in the space below what God does with that item / those items:

Today, I am grateful to God for

1.
2.
3.
4.
5.

> **Breath Prayer**
>
> Speak Your steadfast love
> in the morning, Lord,
> for in You I put my trust;
>
> Teach me the way I should go,
> Lord, for to You I lift up my soul.

Day 2

STARTING POINT In your opinion, where do "planning" and "praying" intersect?

READ the following sets of verses.
   Cluster 1: Proverbs 3:3 – 4; 15:22; 16:3; 16:9; 19:21; 20:18; Psalm 37:3 – 5
   Cluster 2: Luke 22:39 – 44; Matthew 6:7 – 13; 2 Corinthians 1:20 - 22

Cluster 1: What themes do these scriptures have in common? Make a list below.

Where in that list do you see points that apply specifically to you / your questions / your challenges? Go back and underline, circle, or highlight those points.

In Cluster 2, does Jesus's example look like your own prayer life? Discuss.

What does it mean that Jesus is the "yes" to God's promises?

Based on this week's readings so far, what kinds of adjustments might you need to make in order to surrender in prayer / surrender your plans?

ACTION ITEMS

Watch "The War Room." (Priscilla Shirer, 2015) How does this film portray the role of prayer in planning? The role of planning in prayer?

Today, I am grateful to God for

1.
2.
3.
4.
5.

Breath Prayer

Speak Your steadfast love
in the morning, Lord,
for in You I put my trust;

Teach me the way I should go,
Lord, for to You I lift up my soul.

Day 3

STARTING POINT How much scripture reading is enough? How do you know? Do you memorize scripture? Why / why not?

READ Isaiah 55:8 – 11; Matthew 4:1 – 11; 2 Timothy 3:14 – 17; Ephesians 6:13 – 16; Hebrews 4:12

Based on these verses, make a list of the characteristics / qualities of scripture:

What does the prophet Isaiah say about the power of God's word?

How does Jesus demonstrate that power in Matthew's gospel?

What do you think Paul means when he says that scripture is "God-breathed" in 2 Timothy?

What is the difference between "the sword of the Spirit, which is the Word of God" and the other components of the full armor of God as described in Ephesians 6? (Think in terms of defensive vs. offensive purposes.) What does this mean to you, personally?

The author of Hebrews claims that Scripture "judges the thoughts and intentions of the heart." What does that mean for your planning process?

Based on what you've read today, why is it absolutely essential for a Christian to plan according to scriptural guidance and guarantees?

ACTION ITEM Memorize Psalm 119:105 –

"Your word is a lamp to my feet and a light to my path."

Today, I am grateful to God for

1.
2.
3.
4.
5.

Breath Prayer

Speak Your steadfast love
in the morning, Lord,
for in You I put my trust;

Teach me the way I should go,
Lord, for to You I lift up my soul.

Day 4

STARTING POINT John Wesley famously said, "The bible knows nothing of solitary religion." Is that true? Why / why not? Would you characterize your own Christian faith as being more individual, or more part of a community? Discuss.

READ Matthew 18:20; John 15:12 – 13; Acts 2:43 – 47; Hebrews 10:24 – 25; 1 Peter 4:8 – 10; 2 Peter 2:9 – 10

What do these verses have to say about Christian community? Make a list below:

How "connected" are you at church?

Do you have a small group to which you belong?

In which ministry areas are you serving?

Which of your spiritual gifts are you making available for building up of the Body in the context of your own congregation?

ACTION ITEM (pick something you are not already doing):

- Invite someone to go to church with you this coming Sunday.

- If you are not a member already, attend a Sunday School or small group class.

- Explore the mission possibilities at your church. Connect with at least one outreach team. Prayerfully consider committing your service.

- Pray for your pastor(s) and church leaders. Ask God to guide you to serve them in a tangible way.

- Invite two or more friends to go with you to pray a circle around your church property. Ask for God to be glorified in your church community; ask for God to make your church community fruitful for His kingdom.

Today, I am grateful to God for

1.
2.
3.
4.
5.

Breath Prayer

Speak Your steadfast love
in the morning, Lord,
for in You I put my trust;

Teach me the way I should go,
Lord, for to You I lift up my soul.

Day 5

STARTING POINT Make a list of things you do every day. (Brushing your teeth, for example).

READ the following sets of verses.
   Cluster 1: Psalm 68:19; Proverbs 8:32 – 34; Lamentations 3:22 – 23; Luke 9:23
   Cluster 2: Exodus 34:27 – 28; 1 Kings 19:7 – 9; Matthew 4:1 – 2

In the space below, list the ways the verses in Cluster 1 speak to daily / everyday reality:

Given what you have studied this week and last week about your PURPOSE and God's PLAN for your life, brainstorm what new features you will be incorporating into your DAILY life in the following categories.

- Prayer

- Scripture study

- Christian community / church involvement

The verses in Cluster 2 describe pivotal 40-day periods in Scripture: Moses, receiving the Law from God on Mount Sinai; Elijah, receiving encouragement and direction to complete his ministry; Jesus, led by the Spirit, facing temptation prior to launching his earthly ministry.

Compare these biblical accounts of 40-day events with the last 40 days in your own life. What have you received from God? How have you been tested / tempted?

Where is God calling you to go from here?

ACTION ITEM

READ Appendix D, and make a plan for your next devotional reading. Celebrate completing this workbook journey – and commit your plans to the Lord, that they may be established!

Today, I am grateful to God for

1.
2.
3.
4.
5.

Breath Prayer

Speak Your steadfast love
in the morning, Lord,
for in You I put my trust;

Teach me the way I should go,
Lord, for to You I lift up my soul.

Safe

Therefore, since we are surrounded by so great a cloud of witnesses, let us also lay aside every weight and the sin that clings so closely, and let us run with perseverance the race that is set before us, looking to Jesus the pioneer and perfecter of our faith, who for the sake of the joy that was set before him endured the cross, disregarding its shame, and has taken his seat at the right hand of the throne of God. Consider him who endured such hostility against himself from sinners, so that you may not grow weary or lose heart. –*Hebrews 12:1 – 3*

Afterword

As I write this, there are folks in my house making noisy repairs. A historic freeze two months ago resulted in pipes bursting, flooded downstairs bathrooms, and mass displacement. For nine weeks, my dining room has looked a bit like a resale shop, housing stacks of linens and clothes that had to be moved from water-damaged closets. My family has adapted our routine to living in the mess. We have shared the functioning shower upstairs, laughed off the dust and bits of insulation that make their way everywhere, and waited for the day – today! – that people skilled in drywall replacement would arrive to put ceilings and walls back where they are supposed to be.

We have had to wait for others to make these repairs because we were not able to make them ourselves. Simply put, we desired to have the bathrooms fixed and the mess put away but we did not have capacity to make it happen. We needed expert help. Thank God, that help has arrived!

Why is this applicable to a closing message for a Bible study? Because God's heart and God's hands are very like those of the men working in my house right now: God desires, and God is able, to complete the needed repairs remaining in you.

God has begun a colossal work of renovation in you these past weeks. Maybe there's been considerable demolition required, as what was built on false foundations had to be knocked down? Maybe there's been more subtle correctives – a sagging wall strengthened, or a broken window replaced? Regardless of the extent or nature of the work already done in you through this labor of study and devotion, God desires – and God is able – to complete the work.

> **I am confident of this, that the one who began a good work among you will bring it to completion by the day of Jesus Christ.** –*Philippians 1:6*

One of the biggest frustrations of living in a house in urgent need of repair is the waste. A house that can't be used fully is a waste of space and opportunity – uninhabitable rooms, inhospitable conditions. But even once the experts get finished putting rooms back together structurally, there will still be work to do to make rooms habitable and hospitable. Moving piles of stuff, cleaning surfaces, getting organized – making a house ready to be fully useful is a big job. And even when everything is put away and every room is clean, there will be daily work required to keep the house habitable and hospitable. Trash has to be taken out. Dirty laundry has to be done. Dishes have to be washed. Routine chores have to be routine, or the dust will be back.

Very similarly, staying connected to God and growing up into Christ is a big and ongoing job – a job that must be done daily if a Christian is going to experience the peace and purposefulness of living in the center of God's will. You've experienced the way that time spent in God's Word brings about changes and freedom... but if the time in God's Word ceases, those changes and freedoms will, too. Blessedly, there will never be a time when God sees our messes or brokenness as "too much"! Our daily task is to keep inviting God in, giving God access, trusting God to do the whole work – from structural repairs to routine housekeeping.

> **Now to him who by the power at work within us is able to accomplish abundantly far more than all we can ask or imagine, to him be glory in the church and in Christ Jesus to all generations, forever and ever. Amen.** *–Ephesians 3:20 – 21*

A word of caution: we can get used to living in messes. We can accommodate lack of function so long that we cease to perceive the wasted space and opportunity. My family was completely stressed out by living with one shower and disorder everywhere, two months ago... more recently, we've adjusted to the point that it feels "normal" to us. This pattern reflects humanity's highly adaptive nature – a gift from God, but one which we too often misuse. We aren't supposed to get used to chaos, waste, brokenness. We were made for order, purpose, and wholeness!

Moving away from God rarely happens in a single, dramatic event. Most often, it is daily neglect that lulls us, step by step, into squalor. The best offense here is a good defense: investing the daily time with God.

God's pleasure in our devotion and God's patience with our distraction means that we can anticipate new morning mercies, every day, for a lifetime. Your beginning here – your "beginning ... again" here – has been a gift to God of time and focus – but even more than that, it has been a gift to yourself, of receptivity to God's presence. I encourage you: keep giving of yourself, that you may receive of the Lord! The gifts God has in mind for you are beyond our capacity to imagine.

Appendix D contains suggestions for next steps for your walk with God. It's certainly not an exhaustive list of all the wonderful resources out there – just a sampling of some personal favorites of mine. I find that the question of the "best" Bible study has the same answer as the question of the "best" Bible translation: the one you will use, the one you will commit yourself to, that is the "best" one for you.

Thank you for choosing to pursue Christ at a time and in a place when that is a costly, lonely pursuit! Know that you are not alone. The God who made you, called you, and has walked with you to this point will ever abide in you and guide you... all the way home to His embrace.

—*Shannon Vowell*

Appendix A.
Suggestions for Group Study

"Beginning ... *Again*" can easily be used in a group setting. In fact, the workbook was written for group use.

My suggestions below are based on what worked (and what didn't) in those groups; but they are not set in stone. Be creative and apply what will work best for your particular group.

If you use "Beginning ... Again" in a group setting, you will need to make choices regarding leadership and the format of your meeting times. Read on for some suggested ways of approaching leadership and meeting formats, as well as a trouble-shooting list of suggested "do's" and "don'ts".

I. Leadership

If there is <u>one designated leader</u>, then all the structural suggestions below will pertain to him / her primarily.

If <u>leadership is to be shared</u>, there are several ways in which the division of labor could happen:

A. One person leads each week. All leadership responsibilities are managed by one person per week. A rotation of leaders allows everyone opportunity to be participants as well as leaders.

B. A team leads each week. Leadership responsibilities (outlined below) are divided up among group members, and the weekly routine depends on all of those leader-volunteers.

<u>Leadership responsibilities include the following</u>:

1. <u>Time management.</u> Making sure the meeting starts and stops on time; honoring group members' commitments by being punctual.

2. <u>Prayer activity.</u> Praying together, as a group, the assigned prayer for each week. Potentially, coordinating prayer partnerships among group members for ongoing connection between meetings. Keeping the group apprised of prayer requests that emerge in people's lives.

3. <u>Facilitating discussion.</u> Choosing which questions to highlight during group time. Making sure everyone who wants to contribute has the opportunity; making sure no one "dominates" discussion in an unhelpful way.

4. <u>Hospitality.</u> This may or may not apply... but if the group decides to meet at a meal time, the hospitality aspect of leadership will be extensive. Coordinating potluck, making sure there are paper supplies, supervising clean-up afterward.

II. Emphases for Meeting Times

- Do adjust any/all suggested parameters to fit YOUR group's needs.
- Do be attentive to people's time.
- Do emphasize confidentiality: what's shared in the group should stay within the group!
- Do encourage cross-talk outside of group meetings.
- Do hold everyone to a standard of polite listening and careful speech.
- Do defer to scripture on all matters – the only "right answers" are in God's Word!
- Do encourage participation from ALL group members.
- Don't get too far afield. Rabbit trails usually lead nowhere good – avoid them.
- Don't worry. God's in charge, and He knows what He's doing (even when we don't).

Appendix B.
Bible Translations and Why They Matter

Do you speak a foreign language? Many Americans don't.

When I was a kid living in the Netherlands, I felt stupid around kids my age who were already fluent in *several* languages. Routinely, I would stumblingly mumble my few words in Dutch, and then be rescued by their flawless English responses.

Later, studying French in college in Paris, I recall being over the moon when I could understand the bits of francophone conversation I heard while on the metro. Following a French movie without English subtitles was another milestone. And the night I dreamed in French – well. Let's just say it was a heady intellectual victory that wasn't ever repeated.

I also remember the magnetic pull in my heart when I heard spoken English while I was in Paris. Being able to hear and comprehend without the mental work of translation was a sharp, keen pleasure. Listening to English, I was no longer a foreigner – no longer an outsider. It didn't matter if the speakers were strangers to me, we shared a common language and therefore we were comprehensible to each other, and connected.

This emotional / intellectual power is often described in terms of the phenomena of "the language of the heart" or the "mother tongue." Functioning as the parent of our communicational capacity, our "language of the heart" is set early, and we never outgrow it or graduate to another language emotionally – no matter how many other fluencies we may achieve.

This is all background to our discussion about Bible translations because we have to remember that the Bible was NOT written in English. No matter which version you or I pick up in our hands for devotional reading or study, it will be the product of scholars who have done their best to take sentences written in a language that is wholly different from English and make them understandable in English – without sacrificing the original tone or rhythm. That's a tall order. And because of the number of original languages involved (Hebrew, Aramaic, Greek) and their dissimilarity to one another and to English, there has never been and never will be a "perfect" English Bible translation.

But the fantastic news is that, despite the lack of perfection in English Bibles, there is ever-increasing excellence.

Archeological evidence, specialized studies in ancient texts, and painstaking labor on the part of dedicated men and women mean that we have access to Bible translations more precise in their translational accuracy than did English-speaking Christians at any other point in history.

So, which of these excellent English Bibles is the right one for you? In simple terms: the one you will read. However, there are a few distinctions to keep in mind as you mull Bible purchasing.

First, steer clear of "paraphrases" and "interpretive" Bibles – or use them only for devotional pleasure rather than for study. Paraphrases and interpretive versions of scripture are like any other devotional literature – they can be helpful in encouraging and fostering faith. But (like any other devotional literature) they are not authoritative because they contain too much of their human author's imagination and creativity. Examples of this kind of Bible are *The Message* and *The Living Bible*.

Second, decide what you think about gender pronouns. Study Bibles diverge on the proper way to translate what appear as "gender neutral" pronouns in the original languages. For example, the New International Version translates all gender-neutral pronouns in the masculine, while the New Revised Standard Version translates them as both masculine and feminine. Because English doesn't have a gender-neutral pronoun for people ("it" is specifically not a person), either of these translation choices can be valid. Which would work best for you?

Third, beware the baggage of "study notes." A study Bible with an exhaustive concordance, lots of maps, and half of each page taken up with background information and other extras can be a handy tool. But my recommendation would be that you have a Bible for reading and devotional work that is just God's Word – no bells, no whistles, no erudite distractions. It's all too easy to sit down to read the Bible and end up reading the fascinating notes on the Bible found in your Bible, without really reading the Bible itself at all. (I speak from personal experience on this. Ahem.)

Fourth, PLEASE read the Bible in an actual book, made of paper, that you can hold in your hands. I know that "Bible apps" are all the rage, and Kindle and other e-book formats are popular and widespread, but... when seeking to draw close to the Lord who created matter and elevated matter by becoming material Himself, I think it matters to have a material Word. God cannot be digitized; "virtual reality" is not real. A tangible Bible is a reminder that we live in a tangible world and that our Lord invited doubting Thomas, "Put your finger here and see my hands. Reach out your hand and put it in my side. Do not doubt but believe." (John 20:27) And added bonus: the notes you make in the margins of a paper bible will become treasured reminders of God's faithfulness to you over time.

Take care of your eyes – get large print if you need it! Take care of your peace of mind – get whatever kind of publication / cover makes sense for your life. (When my children were little and intent on amiable mass destruction, I used cheap paperback Bibles that could be replaced without blowing the budget.)

Lastly, my personal preferences (that indicate nothing besides my personal preferences): I like the NRSV and the ESV and use both routinely. I also like the NIV.

Appendix C.
Suggestions for Next Steps

Congratulations on completing the 8-week journey of "Beginning ... *Again*"! I pray that your new holy habits are fueling your love of God and neighbor in life-giving ways. And I pray that you are determined to continue seeking God's face daily.

I hope you will hold onto this workbook. In years to come when you look back on what you've written here, you'll be amazed at God's faithfulness to you. How do I know? Because I have a whole shelf of Bible study workbooks, completed at various stages in my faith journey, and I turn to them when I need a reminder of God's faithfulness to *me*.

But right now, you have an exciting decision to make: what will you do *next*? There are so many resources available to you! That can be dazzling and thrilling to contemplate... it can also be overwhelming. So, where do you begin the choosing process?

> **N All Scripture is God-breathed and is useful for teaching, rebuking, correcting and training in righteousness, so that the servant of God may be thoroughly equipped for every good work.** – *1 Timothy 3:16 – 17*

Choosing a Bible Study

What drew you to this study? Doubtless it had something to do with the notion of making a new beginning, not for the first time. As you consider your next study, think in terms of what God has identified to you over the last 8 weeks. Your gifts, your influence, your abilities, your unique insights and experiences – what do you need to nourish and grow?

What follows is by no means an exhaustive list! Please use it as a jumping-off point for your own explorations and adventures.

It's true that not all studies are created equal, and that being sensitive to doctrinal soundness is important. But once you eliminate outright heresy, much of the discernment process proceeds from personal taste... no real "right" or "wrong" answers. So, trust your instincts and the Lord's guidance, and enjoy finding your own favorite authors.

A Collection of Favorites

Maxi Dunnam writes fabulous workbooks. If you are seeking to deepen your prayer life and sense of connection to God in prayer, his *The Workbook of Living Prayer* is a classic work on the topic. I also loved his *Twelve Parables of Jesus* – not a workbook, but a great devotional tool, nonetheless. Dunnam's *The Workbook on Lessons from the Saints* introduces you to some of the great Christian mystics of the centuries… and emphasizes the timelessness of God's truth.

Similarly, two hefty workbooks published by **Richard Foster** via Renovare Resources draw writings from across the Christian ages and make them compellingly relevant to contemporary life. *Spiritual Classics: Selected Readings on the Twelve Spiritual Disciplines* and *Devotional Classics: Selected Readings for Individuals and Groups* will fuel your faith while introducing you to writers whose wisdom and love of God have stood the test of time.

Cynthia Heald writes primarily for women. Her "Becoming a Woman of…" series of workbooks teaches scriptural truth in a gentle, persuasive manner. I particularly benefitted from "Becoming a Woman Who Loves."

Beth Moore writes as if her life depends on it – and then confesses that it does! Her passion for the Lord and her ravenous appetite for God's Word are both contagious. Her workbooks are deep dives into scripture knitted together by Beth's fast-paced and completely unique synthesis of reverence and hilarity. Beth's workbooks have a video component, easily accessible online. My personal favorites are *Jesus, the One and Only*, *Breaking Free*, and *The Patriarchs*.

Henry Blackaby's Experiencing God course is powerful, in whatever format you choose.

Stand-alone books that have enriched my Bible study include **Ann Voskamp**'s *One Thousand Gifts*, **Linda Dillow**'s *Calm My Anxious Heart*, and **Joanna Weaver**'s *Having a Mary Heart in a Martha World*.

Whenever I crave writing that will challenge my brain as it bolsters my faith, I turn to **C.S. Lewis**. His *Mere Christianity* has coaxed more skeptics into the faith than any other book I know. If you are unfamiliar with his writing, or think of him only as the "Chronicles of Narnia" guy, please don't delay: read Lewis and thrive!

For other recommendations, please visit my website at shannonvowell.com and look at the Books page, under Resources.

Dawn

Gratitude

My thanks must begin with my dear friend and co-laborer,
Rebecca Campbell.

Becky, you are the consummate Proverbs 31 woman.

Without your energetic encouragement and persistent vision, there would be no workbook – no website – no blog.

I thank God for you!

This workbook would not be the feast for the eyes that it is without the Spirit-anointed contributions of Sara Joseph, to whom I am eternally thankful. And the expertise and keen eye of Ryan Forsythe made everything work together in a miraculous way, for which I also am grateful beyond words. I also owe a huge debt of gratitude to the generous, wise readers who poured over this work in various stages, making improvements in every area (grammatical to theological)! Thank you, Catherine, Kate, Pat, Jim, Mark, and especially Pam, whose input literally reshaped this book. Sincere thanks also to my brothers and sisters at First Frisco, who prompted this work in the first place.

About the Author

SHANNON VOWELL is a writer, teacher, musician, and mom who delights in working alongside pastor-husband Mark. A nomadic childhood taught her to love travel and adventure, but she didn't learn to love Jesus until later – and now jokes that she's making up for lost time with Him. Shannon holds degrees from Yale and Cambridge. You can read more of her work on her "Why Jesus" website, where she posts a weekly blog at *shannonvowell.com*.

About the Artist

SARA JOSEPH is a painter, sculptor, and author. Born in India, her early art training exposed her to the artistic traditions and rigor of the East. She is the author of the Christian Artist Resource website, which is an online resource for international Christian artists as well as a changing gallery of her own contemporary Christian art. Sara has a BFA from Stella Maris College in Chennai, India. Learn more about her at *Christian-artist-resource.com*.

www.ingramcontent.com/pod-product-compliance
Lightning Source LLC
Chambersburg PA
CBHW051119110526
44589CB00026B/2982